From one Twin Mum to another

An insight into
the complexities
of multiple birth
bereavement

JULIE ANN BRYANT

COPYRIGHT NOTICE
From One Twin Mum To Another: An insight into the complexities of multiple birth bereavement
© Julie Ann Bryant 2022
Cover Image © Julie Ann Bryant 2015
Cover Design: Busybird Publishing 2022
Layout and Typesetting: Busybird Publishing 2022

ISBN
Paperback: 978-1-922954-03-9
Ebook: 978-1-922954-04-6

Except as provided by the Copyright Act 1968, no part of this publication may be reproduced or communicated to the public without the prior written permission of the publisher.

GENRE: Non-fiction. Bereavement, Grief and Loss. Psychology, Self-help.

PERMISSIONS – DISCLAIMER: Written contact was made in 2022 seeking the permission of authors/publishers of other books, together with the organisations mentioned throughout this book. If they do not wish to be included in future editions, then I would welcome contact from them and I will be only too happy to oblige.

Julie Ann Bryant – Email: OzMOST@yahoo.com
Postal: PO Box 246 Unanderra NSW 2526 AUSTRALIA

DEDICATION

*This book is dedicated to the memory
of our twin daughter Meggie,
whose tiny footprints have left
an indelible imprint on our hearts.*

Contents

Foreword i

Preface v

Introduction ix
   Grieving Parents xi
   Social Supports xii
   Professional Supports xii
   Dichotomy xiii
   Disenfranchised xiii
   Desiderium xiv

Part One 1
  Chapter One: When An Unborn Twin Dies 3
    Julie Ann's Story 6
    As Time Went On 9
    Helping Others Understand 11
    Birth Plan 12
      Adjusting To The Loss 12
      Making Memories Of Both Twins Together ... 13
      Other Things To Consider 14
    To the Dad 14
    When Family and Friends Visit 15
    Making Memories While You Are Still Pregnant ... 16
    Naming Your Twins 17
    Getting Through from One Day to the Next ... 18
    Support Person 19
      Prenatal Appointments 19

- Culturally Specific Situations — 19
- Shock and Making Decisions — 20
- Don't Go Flying Under the Radar — 21
- A Note for Health Care Professionals — 22

Chapter Two: Your Grief (Your Love) — 25
- The Maze of Emotions – Making Sense of it All — 31
  - Feeling A Loss Of Status — 33
  - Feeling A Lack Of Meaning Or Purpose — 34
  - Feelings Of Anxiety — 35
  - Feelings Of Failure And Guilt — 35
  - Feeling Helpless And Vulnerable — 37
  - Feeling Isolated — 37
  - Feeling Misunderstood — 38
  - Feeling Pressured — 40
  - Feeling Violated — 41
  - Feeling Anger And Frustration — 42
- Your Grief Will Always Be There — 43
- Unresolved Grief — 43

Chapter Three: You Are Not Alone — 45
- Our Need for People to Gather Around Us — 50
  - Trust Your Gut Feeling — 51
  - Feeling Safe Emotionally — 53
- Helplines — 53
  - PANDA (Perinatal Anxiety and Depression Australia) — 54
  - Red Nose Australia (including SANDS) — 54
  - Lifeline Australia — 55
  - Mensline Australia — 55
  - 13YARN — 55
  - Kids Helpline Australia — 55

Professional Supports	56
Peer Support	57
How We Feel about the Support Around Us	60
The Flip Side	61
Chapter Four: Grief is Survivable	**63**
A Year of Firsts	67
Your Grief Won't Always Be This Raw	68
Keep It Manageable	70
Self-Care	71
Mental Well-Being	74
Physical Well-Being	76
Social Needs	78
Spiritual Connection	78
Memorialising	80
Memory Box	80
Creating Something Meaningful	81
Starting Your Own Traditions	81
Creating A Legacy	82
Conclusion	**85**
Writing and Discussion Prompts	**91**
You and Your Grief	93
Who You Are Because Of Your Grief	94
Your Surviving Twin	94
Your Baby Twin	95
Their Special Days	95
Recommended Reading	**97**
Twin Loss Support	**101**
Organisations	**101**
Australia	103
New Zealand	103
United Kingdom	103

USA	103
PART TWO	**105**
For Those In a Supportive Role	107
Close Social Supports	111
Attending Appointments	113
The Need To Talk	115
The Need To Cry	116
A Loss Is A Loss Is A Loss	117
Extended Social Circles	118
When The Supporter Needs Support	119
Misinterpreting Grief	119
Grief Misconstrued As Not Coping	121
Grief Misconstrued As Being Negative	122
Grief Misconstrued As Jealousy	122
Minimising Grief	124
You're Just Upset	124
You're Feeling Sorry For Yourself	125
You're Just Being Selfish	125
Other Things to Be Aware Of	126
Defaulting To Clichés	126
Pregnancies Don't Come With Guarantees	127
Traditions In The Extended Family Circles	128
Keep Your Focus On The Relationships	129
Be the One Who Remembers	130
Acknowledgements	**131**
About The Author	**135**

Foreword

The juxtaposition of joy and loss entwined together is difficult to balance and make sense of. A new parent is faced with so much when they bring a new baby home, however, when they were supposed to have two babies and one has died, this brings on a mixed set of emotions.

Julie invites the reader to slip down into the well of these mixed emotions. As a psychologist for over 20 years, I had not encountered this complexity until I met Julie. Her book has provided a poignant consideration of a unique side of grief and has taught me so much.

Friends and loved ones don't always know how to reconcile this dichotomy of sad yearning with joy of a new life, or what to say or how to best support grieving parents. This book offers insight and awareness. Reading Julie's work had me reflecting on past miscarriages I had experienced and wishing I had the resource of her insights for my own loss, though different.

With her creativity and easy writing style, Julie's work delicately portrays the dilemma of life and death side-by-side. Julie shares her own poetry and reflections to engage the reader. Her book is beautifully written, practical, easy to read and educational.

Speaking from her lived experience the reader can feel her wisdom and take in the knowledge of someone who has spent a long time reflecting and assisting others who find themselves in the same situation. As an expert with experience, Julie generously and graciously shares all her perspectives and understandings. Her book offers hope, provides writing prompts for journalling one's own story and gives information of where to find support and more resources.

As someone who comes across grief and loss in many forms each day, the worth of this book is immeasurable and I look forward to sharing and recommending the book to those grieving and their families, friends, and professional colleagues.

Julie-Anne Geddes
Psychologist NSW
and author of *Acts of Love*

Preface

Have you ever noticed the language that we use around death? There are so many colloquial terms that we use, perhaps without even giving them a second thought. Terms like "passed away", "gone to heaven" and "gone to sleep" are commonplace. In grief and loss circles, "born sleeping" and "baby born still" are often used to describe miscarriage and stillbirth. Babies who have died are often referred to as "angels" or as "having gone to be with the angels". In multiple birth bereavement, "angel twin" is a very common colloquial term.

I think there are many reasons why we use such language. We may want to soften the blow of the reality by using words that are kind and gentle. Furthermore, we may have anxiety around having such conversations and that's understandable. Talking about death can make us feel uncomfortable, so we will tend to use words that help us have those difficult conversations. However, I can't help but wonder if the language we use around death helps maintain the stigma around losses such as the death of a baby.

If you are at all familiar with the writings of J William Worden, you will likely have read about the "Mediators of Mourning" and the four "Tasks of Mourning". The very first task of mourning that a newly bereaved person goes through is to accept the reality of the death and the second task is to experience the pain of that realisation. The sad reality is that death isn't just for the weekend, it is forever. Whilst we may want to soften the blow with our words, it doesn't change the fact that someone we loved dearly has died and somehow, we have to adjust to living our life without them (the third task) and eventually, we need to create something meaningful out of our loss (the fourth task).

We tend to tiptoe around the reality of death and the language we use reflects that. This is not to say that the language we use should be blunt and insensitive. Rather, it is about being aware that the bereaved person you are talking to is the one who has to do the hard work of grieving and they need to do so in a way that comes naturally to them. Personally, I like to think of it as making your words a hug for the heart. That's exactly what a grieving person needs. What they need is to be heard, to know you understand that they are in deep emotional pain, to be validated in their loss, supported as they grieve and loved the whole way through.

Above all, with this book I want to create a safe place where we can look together at the complex issues of multiple birth bereavement. Together, we can help break the stigma that has surrounded pregnancy loss and infant death for way too long.

With warm regards,

Julie Ann

Introduction

This book is written with a very specific audience in mind and targeted at a very specific, traumatic time in their lives. For these people, what should be a wonderfully happy experience of a twin pregnancy and parenthood becomes fraught with the uncertainty of what lies ahead. Instead of planning for everything in two's, life begins to be taken one tentative step at a time. This is a long, emotional journey and whether you are the expectant parents or in a supportive role, I want to reach out to you through the pages of this book to reassure you that you will get through this.

Grieving Parents

First and foremost, this book is for grieving parents who have a surviving child of a multiple pregnancy. If this is the reason why you hold this book in your hands, then I am so very sorry for your loss. You loved your babies from the moment you learnt of their existence. You had already started planning your future with them. You had developed a strong and beautiful emotional connection with your babies. Your loss is profound. You have lost a part of yourself and a part of your future. Losing a baby twin results in a complex grieving process and I hope I can help you understand the nature of this very complex grief. I also hope I can help you focus on your own self-care and help you think about ways to enable your own way of coping as you navigate your way through these early days of loss.

You will note, that when differentiating between your twins, I refer to each twin as either your *surviving twin* or your *baby twin*. My reasoning for this is that your baby who has died will always be remembered as a baby, whereas, your surviving twin will age and it will be necessary to view them in the context of their changing age. (Please also note that my references to twins is understood to include higher-order multiple pregnancies.)

To the dads, whilst this book is written from my own perspective as a mum, I realise that your grief is often overlooked while at the same time a lot of expectations are placed on your shoulders. All the way through this book, I have used the terms "grieving parents/bereaved parents" and in doing so, I hope you will feel included in the conversation.

Social Supports

Secondly, you may be a family member or close friend of the grieving parents and are wanting to support them but are not sure how to do so. Your emotional connection to the baby twin will differ to that of the parents. You may struggle with understanding the depth of pain the grieving parents are experiencing. It is my hope that this book – and especially the final chapter in Part Two, which I have written with you in mind – will provide an insight into what your loved ones are going through as they experience the overwhelming waves of their grief.

Professional Supports

Thirdly, you may be a health care professional or a mental health care professional with newly bereaved parents in your care. Several times throughout this book, I encourage bereaved parents (and their social supports) to tap into professional supports when they need to. It is my hope that this book will also be a valuable resource for you as a health care professional. Whether you are a GP, midwife, nursing staff, hospital social worker, baby health clinic nurse, grief counsellor, psychologist or obstetrician, grieving parents will be looking to you to help guide them through the early days of their loss. I hope this book helps you to do that.

If I could use three words to describe the experience of multiple birth bereavement, those words would be dichotomy, disenfranchised and desiderium.

Dichotomy

The entire experience of losing a twin is one of coexisting opposites – of life and death, hope and despair, joy and sadness. It is bittersweet. In the very early days of grief, this dichotomous existence is very perplexing. Just how do you experience joy and sadness simultaneously? And just as perplexing, how do you separate them when the feelings are so overwhelming?

Disenfranchised

Multiple birth bereavement is a disenfranchised type of grief, that is, a grief that is often not socially recognised or supported. The image of a mother holding her baby is usually one of joy and hope. Multiple birth bereavement is unique because the grief of parents with a surviving twin is often overlooked.

At first glance, the title of this book "From One Twin Mum To Another" could be understood to refer to one twin mum conversing with another, and in one sense it is. There is, however, a much deeper meaning to it. It is a reference to the disenfranchisement that many grieving multiple birth parents experience as they transition from a tangible/social recognition as the parents of twins to a more private, yet ongoing, definition of themselves as the parents of twins. Although their surviving child's birth status is as one of twins, they are often no longer socially recognised as such. In 2001, in the very early days of my own loss, I wrote these words and they have become timeless for me through the years: "I am still the mother of twins – just not in the way I had hoped for or anticipated."

Desiderium

Originating from Latin, the word desiderium describes the deep sense of desire and longing experienced as a part of grief. Over the last 20 years of offering peer support to other families raising the surviving child of a multiple pregnancy, I have been privileged to observe the deep sense of loss and yearning that is expressed when parents talk about their baby twin who has died. Yet there is another layer to the loss for the grieving parents as well. Not only have they lost their child, but their surviving twin has also lost their sibling, their womb-mate. As parents watch their surviving twin grow and reach milestones through the years, their loss and yearning is often accompanied by wondering what it might have been like to have both twins together.

As you read through this book, keep these three words in your mind. They underscore the themes of this very complicated grief and the subsequent need for appropriate professional and social supports.

Part One

Chapter One

When An Unborn Twin Dies

From my poetry collection © 2013

You are always just a whisper away,
This thought brings me comfort
as I think of you each day.
Sometimes I sense you're so very near
and when I whisper your sweet name
I am sure that you hear.
I've often wondered what might have been
to have you here with us...
I close my eyes and try to visualise
my girl, now almost twelve –
and yet you will forever be
that precious tiny baby,
my sweet little Meggie,
my beautiful untouched pearl...
I wonder how tall you'd be,
how long would be your hair,
Of how your eyes would sparkle
as you laugh and smile.
I imagine every detail of your face
And capture that image in my mind's eye
if just for a little while.
You were so much a part
of our hopes and dreams as a family,
And while you're gone you are still here,
You have a special place in my heart.

Julie Ann's Story

"Congratulations Julie, you're pregnant!". I was speaking on the phone with one of the IVF nurses. I had been down to pathology early that morning for a Beta test and had been pondering for hours: "Will I be drinking mineral water tonight or wine?". It had been an exciting but anxious two weeks following the IVF transfer. Our two babies were five-day-old blastocysts on the day of the transfer and we had seen them magnified hundreds of times up on the screen in the operating theatre. In their pre-embryonic state, our "best" blastocyst was almost ready to hatch out of the zona. It was amazing to see both our babies up there looking so promising when most parents don't get to see their babies via ultrasound for another month or so at least! We were so pleased we had chosen the five-day transfer – it gave us peace of mind to know that our babies were growing and developing under the watchful eye of the embryologist.

For the next three weeks we anxiously awaited our turn for the "baby count" ultrasound. I was now in my 7th week of pregnancy and this would be the last examination I would have as an IVF patient. We even dared to hope that both of our babies had implanted. When the time came we saw a little cashew-shaped body with a strong little heart beating away in there. That was our first glimpse of our precious "Twin 1". The sonographer then did what I thought was all the imaging necessary and I resigned myself to the thought that only one of our babies was still with us, so can you imagine my joy when I saw her type "Twin 2" on the screen. It was just a magical moment and I felt so very blessed to be pregnant with twins! Twins!! All of the pain and disappointment of so many years of primary infertility and failed treatment cycles just seemed to melt away in that instant.

As the weeks went by I couldn't believe how well I felt. I'd had nausea although no morning sickness. I was swimming most days and felt so very healthy and happy. I was then given a referral for the mid-pregnancy Level 2 morphological sonogram. Despite the uncomfortably full bladder, I was buzzing with excitement as I arrived for my appointment. It was wonderful to see our "Twin A" on the screen, perfectly formed and as the sonographer kept on saying, "yep, he's definitely a boy!" He didn't like the probe bearing down on him and kept wriggling around as if to say, "Hey mum, what's going on out there?!" The sonographer explained everything to us as he went along. We saw his brain, eyes, fingers and toes, stomach, bladder, heart and spine. We were given such a wonderful glimpse of our little boy.

I was just quietly marvelling at everything we had seen so far when the sonographer looked at me and said, "Julie, I don't know how to tell you this but your Twin B is a lot smaller than Twin A." It took a few moments for his words to sink in. When I asked him, "can you see a heartbeat?", I instinctively already knew the answer. He said he couldn't and that he was really sorry. He went to consult with the radiologist.

I lay there with tears streaming down my cheeks as my husband held my hand and just kept on passing me more tissues. It felt like forever before the sonographer returned to the ultrasound room with the radiologist. The radiologist was saying there were lots of issues for me now and he'd ring the obstetrician at the hospital but I was only half hearing him. I was in disbelief that one of my babies had died. I have since replayed that moment over in my mind a thousand times and each time I think how nothing can prepare you for being told that your baby is dead. I lay there stunned, thinking, "I don't want to lose both of my babies!" This was the day my life changed forever.

We saw the obstetrician the following day. The cause of Meggie's death was indeterminate and the radiologist's report described her as "sonographically normal". He gave us a glimmer of hope in saying he was confident I'd carry both babies to term. He did, however, explain that I could go into premature labour at any time with the possibility of losing both babies so, half-way through my pregnancy, my hospital bag was packed.

Mentally, the rest of the pregnancy was extremely difficult. It is very hard to reconcile the joy and hope you have for one baby with the overwhelming sense of grief and loss you have for the other baby. Those emotions are two extremes, exact opposites, and although there did not seem to be any balance in-between, I had to live with them simultaneously. For the remainder of the pregnancy I had fortnightly sonograms to monitor the condition of both babies.

The sonographer would always ask if I wanted to see my other baby and I would always say yes. It was comforting to see Meggie was still there with us. I would drink in those images of her, trying to imprint them on my memory, not knowing if this would be the last time I would see her. Whilst I grieved so very deeply for Meggie, I also felt that for our surviving twin's sake I had to focus on him and keep on daring to hope he would grow as he should and make it to term.

As Time Went On

It may sound strange for me to say that when a baby dies, we lose a part of our future. It doesn't seem possible when the future hasn't happened yet… however, this is the nature of the maternal and paternal bond we have with our unborn child. We discover we are pregnant and we begin to imagine what our life will be like with this child. We imagine hearing their first cry, holding them in our arms for the first time, seeing their first smile, hearing their first giggle… and their first word, watching them take that first tentative step, waving them goodbye on their first day of school. That is the future that we lose – our hopes and dreams of what might be.

By the time my twin pregnancy was confirmed, I had already started to develop a strong maternal, emotional attachment to both of my babies. With a long history of infertility and failed treatment cycles, it had taken me about 15 years to get to this point of my life. "Double the trouble" was often quoted to me in jest, to which I would reply, "No, double the joy." I had already spent several years imagining myself as a mum and with the nature of IVF treatment cycles, I knew that I had a higher chance of conceiving a multiple pregnancy. So, when those two little hearts beating under mine were confirmed, they became my joy, my hope and my dream for the future.

Countless times through the years I have been asked how I coped for the second half of my pregnancy, knowing that Meggie had died… knowing I would have to give birth to her alongside her twin brother. My usual response was that I gathered my strength and wits about me as I mentally prepared myself for what lay ahead. The complicated thing about that though was that there were so many unknowns. Not only had I never experienced anything remotely like that before, but I also did not know of anyone else who had experienced a twin pregnancy just like mine either. Nobody in my circles of extended family or friends knew what I was going through or what my emotional needs were in order to support me. Furthermore, I felt that many health care professionals also did not understand the emotional impact of the complexities arising from my pregnancy. In my previous work as a medical transcriptionist, I had typed countless obstetric reports and yet I had no recollection of ever transcribing a report of a twin pregnancy like mine. These realisations made my situation feel quite unique, very rare. There is nothing quite like the feeling that NOBODY around you understands what you are going through – especially when it is a complicated and difficult journey. It is an excruciatingly lonely feeling.

I did gain some comfort and reassurance from being monitored weekly by the hospital prenatal clinic. Carrying an unborn twin who has died increases the risk of blood clots for the mother, especially as the pregnancy progresses. As Meggie died mid-way through my pregnancy, I was monitored regularly with DIC screens, a blood test to detect any abnormal blood clotting (DIC is a medical abbreviation for Dissemination Intravascular Coagulation). Having worked for a group of radiology doctors for over 12 years, I was used to hearing medical terminology used in a clinical manner, although it was hard not to feel alarmed when hearing those terms being used about me! I worked hard not to worry myself unnecessarily over the potential complications of the pregnancy (although it was always in my thoughts) and I did my best to just focus on getting through the pregnancy week-by-week and making it to my next prenatal appointment. The hospital Registrar who assessed me most weeks was very kind and thoughtful, and he would let me hear my surviving twin's heartbeat. I found this very reassuring, as well as seeing both babies on the screen during ultrasound. These little things are what helped me mentally prepare myself for their births and it gave me hope to hang on and get through each day of the pregnancy.

Helping Others Understand

Those early months at home with our newborn twin son kept me busy as I attended to his needs around the clock and adjusted to life as a first-time mum. Yet, as the weeks and months went on, I felt like I was the only person who had experienced the death of an unborn twin, carrying both babies to near full-term. That realisation made me yearn all the more for contact with others who, through their own lived experiences, understood what I had been through.

Fast-forward to when my surviving twin was a few years old. I was very thankful when some health care professionals did reach out to me, expressing their interest in managing complicated, high-risk twin pregnancies like mine. In my experience, health care professionals do often welcome the insights of the bereaved parents themselves – after all, they want to provide the best care they can to their patients. As a result I have had the privilege of sharing with them not only the story of my twin pregnancy but also my thoughts – as outlined in the pages that follow – on how to support patients in their care going forward.

There are lessons I learnt either during my own twin pregnancy or with the benefit of hindsight. Looking back to those early days of my loss, my one enduring thought is of how fleeting the window is for some opportunities. If things aren't carefully considered in advance, then those opportunities may be lost –

and, sadly, they are gone forever. This is often where regrets run deep for grieving parents, which can subsequently complicate their grieving process. Listed below are some thoughts that may be of help while you are awaiting the birth of your twins.

Birth Plan

The most important thing is to have a birth plan in place, developed in advance together with your partner and discussed with your midwife. It will take a lot of pressure off you to have things all thought through and written down in your birth plan of ahead of time.

Adjusting To The Loss

If you stay in the maternity ward for a few days, you may want to ask about the availability of a single-bed room. You will need privacy as you spend time with each baby. Regardless of whether you stay at the hospital or choose to go home, you may want to consider having the first day after your twins' births "visitor-free" just so that you can have some privacy as you adjust to the reality of your situation.

Those early days with your surviving twin will be filled with a whole range of emotions. There will be some moments of joy and celebration and other moments of grief and sadness. You may find immense comfort in being able to hold your surviving twin. Allow yourself to feel whatever emotion you need to at any given time. It is understandable that you will feel sad. It is also okay to feel happy. Don't feel guilty about that.

Similarly, spend as much time as you want with your baby twin who has died. Your baby can be wrapped in warm blankets before being brought to you. It is impossible to predict the appearance of a baby who has died prior to the birth and fear of the unknown may be very real to you. This is very understandable. Don't be afraid to touch and hold your baby. Every moment that you spend with him/her will become a precious memory. This is a special time and no grieving parent that I am aware of has ever had regrets about spending this time with their baby twin who has died.

Making Memories Of Both Twins Together

Your birth plan should include opportunities for making memories of your twin who has died and of both twins together. This is a very common regret that multiple birth parents have, that both babies weren't held together or photographed as an intact set of multiples. This can be a special time of making memories while the opportunities are there.

As well as photographs and videos, give careful consideration as to what will be helpful for you in the way of other special keepsakes – things like the cot tags indicating "Twin 1" and "Twin 2" together with foot-prints, hand-prints and locks of hair. Later, you may want to put these special keepsakes into a Memory Box. In a very real sense, you are fitting a lifetime of memories into the time you will have with your babies – both as you await their birth and once they are born.

It is a sad realisation that the duration of time you have with both babies together will never be enough. This is when tangible reminders of your babies as an intact set of twins will become immeasurably precious through the years.

Other Things To Consider

If your baby twin has died earlier in the pregnancy, the baby may "vanish" into the placental membranes as the pregnancy progresses to term. Following the birth, placental examination may be possible and this is something you may wish to discuss with your midwife.

For very small babies, you may wish to consider having him/her cremated with the placenta. As well as a beautiful symbol of both twins together, this will also provide you with enough ashes to keep or scatter. Again, this is something you may wish to discuss with your midwife.

If your baby twin reached 20 weeks' gestation or had a minimum birth weight of 400g, you can register him/her with the Registry of Births, Deaths and Marriages in the Australian state or territory in which you live. This also means that the birth certificate for your surviving twin will acknowledge his/her status as one of twins.

If your baby twin died before 20 weeks' gestation and weighed less than 400g, you can apply for a "Recognition of Early Pregnancy Loss" certificate, which will be an important acknowledgement of his/her existence for you now and for your surviving twin in the future. (An online search with the keywords "certificate recognition early pregnancy loss" should provide you with the government website and link for your Australian state or territory.)

To the Dad

The dreams we have for our children is a shared dream between both partners and it is important to acknowledge that your world and your dreams, have also been shattered. You are also on the roller-coaster ride of emotions as you navigate your way through an unknown world. You may feel a need to be strong in order to provide support and protection for your partner, the surviving twin and other children. You may also feel a sense of helplessness, watching your partner deal with the complications of the pregnancy as it progresses to term.

It may seem that you and your partner are on different pages of your grief and that is okay. You will both grieve individually but you'll get through it together. Our society tends view grief in a negative light, and I think this is especially true for men, and yet grief is our natural response when we experience such a profound loss. Can I just encourage you to grieve in a way that feels natural for you and urge you to reach out for support when you need to.

When Family and Friends Visit

Think about how you want to handle it when your family and friends fuss over your surviving twin. People may hesitate to mention your baby twin who has died. Though being well-meaning, they may not want to upset you. What they may not understand, though, is that it is more upsetting if you feel you're not "allowed" to talk about both of your twins.

If you are finding it difficult to talk to lots of different people individually, you may want to pre-emptively consider writing an "open letter" to family and friends. This may be helpful in increasing their awareness and understanding of the situation through your eyes, especially as you become more aware of your own needs and how you would like to handle your situation.

Making Memories
While You are Still Pregnant with Your Twins

There are also memories that you can make of your twins while you are still pregnant with them. At your routine ultrasound appointments, the sonographer may provide you with sonogram images or videos of your babies. Take a photo of your toes peeking below your pregnant belly while you can still see them. If you have older children, include them in your progress photos as your belly grows.

Write love-letters to your babies. Make a photo album or scrapbook that tells the story of your twins. Buy a piece of jewellery to wear that has special significance for you. Create a playlist of special songs that remind you of love and life and may help you to think of your twins in a comforting way. You may want to plant a tree or build a special remembrance garden. You may even want to put a plaque there with your baby twin's name on it or place a small statue there.

There are so many beautiful things that you can do to create memories with your twins while you are still pregnant and I am hoping you will think of other things that are especially meaningful for you that I haven't thought of here. It is important to make beautiful memories while you are still pregnant, because these are the things that will help you hang on.

As your pregnancy progresses to term, you may also develop little ways of communicating with your surviving twin. Make sure you write about these special moments in your journal. A favourite memory I have of my twin pregnancy is in the third trimester, where every evening after dinner I would sit to watch some TV. Inevitably, my surviving twin would jut his little bottom out from under my ribs and I would soothe him to sleep by rubbing his back.

If I stopped the belly rubs too soon he would kick me hard in protest! Eventually he would settle in for a nice, long sleep. For the rest of the pregnancy, this was our nightly ritual and it continued after my twins were born. As a newborn, his little wriggles and squirms were all so familiar to me. It is my favourite memory of that time, having to rub his back to settle him to sleep. This is a memory that always makes me smile.

Naming Your Twins

If you haven't already, then I would encourage you to name both of your babies. Even if they haven't been born yet, naming your baby twin who has died is a beautiful way to acknowledge his/her humanity. It may be difficult to choose a name to begin with and some parents prefer to keep certain names for their future living children (and that's understandable!).

Choosing a name for your children is a very personal decision. In this situation, where so many other things feel wrong, deciding on a name will just feel right. Making choices like this is something you do actually have control over and once you do settle on a name for your baby twin who has died, their name will become the one thing that is truly theirs.

Meggie was named in honour of the doctor who set me on the path to motherhood. Margaret is the English variant of the Celtic name Megan, and both names mean "pearl". After the birth, when I saw Meggie's tiny and frail but perfectly formed body, her skin was very pearl-like, which added to the significance and beauty of it for me.

Getting Through from One Day to the Next

As bereaved parents, you need validation of your loss and support as you mentally prepare yourselves for the birth of your babies. During the pregnancy you and your partner will both be profoundly affected emotionally as you grapple with the impending live birth and stillbirth of your twins. You will both be living with those extremes of joy and sadness, and for the expectant mum, also contending with all of the pregnancy hormones.

Whilst awaiting the birth you may have days when you experience anger or frustration. This is very understandable considering you are in a situation over which you have little or no control. You may also struggle with feeling it's not fair and you may experience fear of the unknown as you try to anticipate the birth of both babies. You may be fearful that your surviving twin could also die. It may help to talk these things over with someone, whether that be a trusted friend or relative, or your GP or other health care professional.

As your pregnancy progresses, you may also withdraw from some social contexts, needing to focus on yourself and rest as much as possible (remember that grieving is physically exhausting, not to mention latter pregnancy!).

Alternatively, you may be using coping mechanisms that give the impression you are going okay. You may be staying strong and stoic as you await your babies' births. People were often taken aback at how well I seemed to be coping. In actual fact, I was just coping and getting through each day as best I could. For the days when I needed to, I would pace myself hour-by-hour and sometimes even breath-by-breath. This helped me do the everyday things that needed to be done, like grocery shopping or paying bills, and it helped provide me with some "time-out" from the intensity of my emotions. Being "strong" was my way of coping – it was necessary for my mental and emotional well-being until I was ready to deal with my grief. I was also worried about the impact the stress would have on my unborn surviving twin and tried to remain as calm and positive as possible. Appearing to be strong was a double-edged sword, however, as it served to deny me the emotional support I so desperately needed.

Support Person

Prenatal Appointments

As it may be daunting to attend your prenatal appointments alone, it is worthwhile considering having a support person who can attend the prenatal appointments with you. They may be your partner or a trusted relative or friend. For the duration of your pregnancy, questions will likely arise and you may want to write them down to take with you to your appointment so you won't have to worry about forgetting to mention important things. Having someone there, who you know and trust, can also help calm your anxiety. They can be helpful in remembering things too. It also means that you will have someone to talk things over with, on the way to and from the appointment.

Culturally Specific Situations

If you identify as an Indigenous Australian, you may want to consider having a support person who can help facilitate culturally-appropriate observations and practices that are of great meaning and significance for you and your family. I want to acknowledge that, as a First Nations person, you are grieving for many things and how important it is that you say goodbye and honour your baby twin in your own way. I hope that this will become a beautiful part of the ongoing story you have to tell your loved ones, and especially your surviving twin.

Similarly, if you are of another culture, it is my sincere hope that you will have a support person to help ensure the birth, as a memory-making experience, is of great meaning and significance to you and your family.

Shock and Making Decisions

No matter when your baby twin has died, you will most likely experience shock. You may have had very little time in which to make decisions about, for example, an emergency caesarean section, emergency surgery on your newborn surviving twin or the withdrawal of life support.

You may have to make decisions about autopsies – full body, partial body or, in some instances, even placental. In this state of shock, you may also have to make other important decisions, for example, about funeral arrangements.

In my talks with health care professionals, I have compared this type of shock with a day-surgery procedure where the patient is required to sign a form declaring they will not, amongst other things, make significant decisions for 24 hours after having the anaesthetic. Bereaved parents don't have this luxury – they have to make the most difficult decisions concerning their baby/s whilst they are in a severe state of shock.

Don't Go Flying Under the Radar

If you have a history of a diagnosed mental illness, then it is imperative that you talk about it to the health/mental health professionals who are managing your twin pregnancy. You don't want to go flying under the radar with your mental well-being. It is possible that clinical depression, for example, or postnatal depression with a previous pregnancy, etc, can recur concurrently with your grief, complicating and prolonging your grieving process. It is really important for you to seek and make use of the professional supports you need for your ongoing well-being.

Similarly, even if you don't have a prior mental health history but have an inkling, a sense, that something doesn't feel quite right, then I would strongly encourage you to talk to your health/mental health professionals about what might be going on for you. It will not be an easy conversation for you to have, however, it is an important one. I want to reassure you that there is no shame in struggling with your mental health, especially at a traumatic time like this, and if your health care professionals are aware that you are struggling in this regard, then extra help and support will be made available to you. I hope that as a result of that conversation, you will feel relieved and proud of yourself for being brave enough to elicit the extra support you need.

Be self-aware and be diligent with your mental health because you deserve to feel well and to grieve well, and you want to be able to enjoy all of those beautiful, sweet, special moments with your surviving twin as you watch him/her grow. Don't let flying under the radar rob you of that.

A Note for Health Care Professionals

If you are a health care professional don't wait for the parents to ask for support. Encourage them to talk to their GP regarding a mental health plan and referral for ongoing grief counselling, especially where there is a pre-existing history of mental illness. With everything that they have had happen in so short a period of time, and as they process the trauma of their experience more, they will likely become more ready to talk about it. It is not uncommon for grieving parents to remember the events of their twins' birth as fragmented memories that can resurface several weeks or even months later. The therapeutic benefit of talking their grief and trauma through with a mental health professional will likely help them remember more of those fragmented memories and process them in a more sequential way.

A further complicating factor in the parents' grief may occur when their baby twin's life ended as a result of a decision they had to make on medical grounds. For example, this may be through the withdrawal of life-support or through surgical intervention for selective reduction, cord ligation or the separation of conjoined twins. Despite having the knowledge and understanding the medical advice that there was no other choice, such decisions will weigh heavily on a parent's conscience and they may struggle with deep feelings of guilt and remorse.

The grieving parents may find that many people they come into contact with will encourage them to focus only on their surviving twin. Whilst we all have a need to hang onto hope – and focusing on the surviving twin helps us do that – the trauma associated with their baby twin who has died can easily be overlooked. Grief counselling for parents can help facilitate them talking about their needs with regard to their baby twin who has died, without the pressure of focusing only on their surviving twin. Grief counselling will also give them a safe place in which to analyse the trauma of their experience and the impact it has had on them.

Finally, when the babies are born continue to refer to them as twins – especially the surviving twin. Encourage the parents not to be afraid of their baby twin who has died. Remember, they will be looking to you to give them guidance.

Chapter Two

Your Grief (Your Love)

~~~~~~~~~~~~~~~~

From my poetry collection © 2013

I think the greatest myth, when it comes to grief,
Is that time heals all things.
It does not.
Grief is a process
that we have to work our way through.
We have to engage ourselves in that process,
expressing our grief in a way that is natural
and congruent to how we feel.
This is, I believe, where the healing process begins –
where we learn to honour our loss,
create meaning out of it
and embrace what life has yet to offer.
At some point or other,
grief will be a part of our life experience.
None of us are exempt from experiencing loss
and the feelings of grief that will naturally follow.
How we grieve is individual.
We can't ignore it or run away from it.
Our grief is an expression of our love.
Allow it…
Honour it…
Understand it…
And seek to create meaning out of it.

Experiencing loss and the subsequent grief is something we will each go through during the course of our lives. Our experience of grief will be unique to us. There are many contributing factors which will influence both our understanding and our experience of grief.

American psychologist J William Worden explains these factors as the "Mediators of Mourning". In a nutshell, the Mediators offer an in-depth look at our relationship with the person who has died, taking into consideration the emotional attachment we have developed with them and the nature of their death.

This is all put into context with other factors, such as our personality, how we have grieved previous losses, the social supports we do (or don't) have, and other complicating factors that may occur as a result of the death. Quite simply, the Mediators of Mourning help to explain why we grieve the way we do.

I have learnt over the years that the grieving process is far more complex than a series of "stages" that one merely goes through. There are various stage theories of grief and most people will be familiar with them.

However, to think of grief in terms of stages is very limiting because it implies that grief is something you will "get over" and with that is the expectation that the grief will pass quickly. Nothing could be further from the truth.

Again, Worden's approach to the grieving process resonates a lot with me. As well as the Mediators of Mourning, Worden has identified the four "Tasks of Mourning":

1. accepting the reality of the loss
2. experiencing the pain of our grief
3. adjusting to life without our loved one and
4. memorialising our loved one.

I like to think of the Tasks of Mourning as emotional and cognitive milestones we reach as we journey through our grief. Imagine with me that we are standing on the bank of a river and we have to get to the other side. Our only way of accomplishing this is to go through the water. We will have to navigate our way over rocks in some places and through deep water in other places. Sometimes we will have to swim against the current and it will be exhausting. At other times the current will take us where we don't want to go and we will struggle to stay focused on getting to the other side. There will be times when we think we won't make it, that it's too hard. Yet, eventually – with courage and determination we never knew we possessed – we will reach the other side of the river.

Grief is like that. I have often said that grief is not something we get over – rather it is a process that we must go through. It's not optional. And as we navigate our way through the waters of our own grief, we work towards completing those four emotional and cognitive tasks along the way. When we are safe on the other side of the river, we may find there are days when we need to revisit any one of those four emotional tasks – the one difference will be that we now know we will survive and that we will re-emerge with a renewed sense of self, autonomy and purpose.

So what is grief? Grief is our emotional response to a significant loss. It is really just an expression of our love. It leaves us feeling heartbroken and so very sad because the one we want to give that love to is no longer there. We feel heartbroken because all our hopes and dreams for our twins together will never be realised. With multiple birth bereavement there is an added layer of "desiderium", that deep sense of yearning and longing. We have our surviving twin. As we watch them grow up before our very eyes, in one sense it's not hard to imagine another child – their twin sibling – by their side. There's a part of us that will always wonder what might have been and what our twins' relationship would have been like if they had been able to grow up together. Watching our surviving twin go through life alone can make us wonder all the more.

When we face such unusual circumstances, it helps to have our feelings normalised – the situation itself is not "normal" but our responses to it are totally understandable. During the course of grieving, we experience a range of emotional responses. Let's now take a look at some of the things that many grieving parents experience during those first few years when their grief is acute.

The Maze of Emotions
– Making Sense of it All

With time and care, having accepted the reality of our loss and experienced the emotional pain of that realisation, we slowly start to adjust to a "new normal" and can memorialise our baby twin in a meaningful way. I believe we go through grief intuitively and spontaneously, in our own way and time, and that it can be neither rushed nor dismissed.

Sadness is a natural response to loss. Not only has your much-loved and much-wanted baby twin died, but the future you had anticipated – with your child in it – has now changed. Furthermore, you now have to find a way to reconcile the future you thought you had with the future you now have. That realisation can evoke deep feelings of sadness and our tears are a natural expression of that deep sadness. It is okay to feel sad and cry. I hope that at those times, someone will be there to nurture and care for you.

Multiple birth bereavement is a complex loss because not only are you grieving for your baby twin who has died, but you are also taking care of the needs of your surviving twin. Grief can be all-consuming and exhausting. Looking after a newborn baby is also all-consuming and exhausting. There is little relief from either and yet you have to cope with both realities simultaneously.

In the pages that follow are other emotions that you may experience as a part of your grief. Please note, this list is by no means exhaustive and there may be other things that you experience that are not included. This list is intended to help explain why grief makes us feel the way we do. As you look through the list in the coming pages, please consider the following:

- What are your specific needs and what are the ways in which they could be met?
- What has helped you in the past when navigating your way through difficult times? This will be a good starting point in working your way through your feelings now.

Feeling A Loss Of Status

Death takes away our status as the parents of our child in a tangible sense. In a multiple pregnancy, there is also a loss of status as the parents of twins. A big fuss can occur when a twin pregnancy is announced. People often joke with first-time parents that you have no idea of what's about to hit once your babies are born. They may congratulate you on being so clever as to conceive twins and they may come bearing baby gifts of everything in twos. It can be a very exciting time.

All of that excitement shuts down when an unborn twin dies and this understandable response to their new circumstance of loss is absolutely devastating for the expectant parents. Running parallel with that previous excitement was the acknowledgement of the twin pregnancy and this acknowledgement often shuts down at the same time. In many cases, people around you may shift their attention towards your surviving twin. Some people may even apologise for being excited that you were pregnant with twins (note the past tense). It may not even occur to them that yours is still a high-risk, complicated twin pregnancy.

This is what I mean when I say that this kind of grief is disenfranchised – it is often not recognised as a "real" loss and therefore also not supported in an appropriate way. At the very time when you need extra support and understanding from those around you, some people will find your circumstances too confronting to think about. For some, it will be far easier to default to thinking about your pregnancy as now being a "singleton" pregnancy. However, the reality is not that you have just suddenly, mysteriously become "unpregnant" with twins – you still have to carry your babies to term and to mentally prepare yourself for their live-birth and stillbirth. The loss of this social recognition and status as the parents of twins can thus be quite profound.

It helps grieving parents enormously to be acknowledged as the parents of twins – both before and after their babies are born. It also helps when their surviving child's multiple birth status as one of twins is acknowledged.

Feeling A Lack Of Meaning Or Purpose

Death doesn't discriminate despite the "natural order" of things being that we are born, live to a ripe old age, then die. Our children aren't supposed to die before we do. We bring them into the world, wanting to love and protect them and to be there to watch them grow up. In a perfect world, that's how it would be.

The death of a baby can leave us questioning many things. It may leave us questioning the meaning of life. We may challenge, for the first time in our life, the beliefs that we have always held. We may ask "Why did this happen to us?" We may be left feeling bewildered about who we are in the face of this loss, and of who we are becoming. A big part of the hard work of grief we have to do is in coming to a place of peace as we grapple with these questions.

It may help to memorialise your baby in a meaningful way which enables you to remain emotionally connected with him/her. With time, you will find it is okay to give yourself permission to go on with life. You know that your baby will always have their special place within your heart and in your family throughout the years. A bit further down the track you may even create a legacy in your baby's honour. In the early days of your loss, it may help you to find a creative outlet for expressing your grief, for telling your story. You could keep a journal or write poetry, do photography and create a scrapbook, engage in art, or anything else that helps some peace enter in.

Feelings Of Anxiety

Who wouldn't feel anxious? Your whole world has been turned upside down and you are now navigating your way through uncharted territory. Everything you had anticipated and hoped for has changed and as you navigate your way through this unknown reality, you might well feel anxious. You may worry about yourself. You may worry about your partner. You may worry about your surviving twin. You may worry about the rest of the pregnancy. You may worry about the birth. You may worry about your other children. You may worry about the unknowns.

Anxiety can express itself in a few different ways. You may worry about the "what if's" of your situation, searching your soul for answers. You may feel unusually "highly strung". You may have panic attacks in specific situations. You may feel so anxious that you want to avoid certain situations... or seek to control them. When you consider all you have been through in so short a period of time, feeling anxious is very understandable.

When you become aware of your anxious thoughts, take some deep slow breaths and remind yourself that you are making a huge effort to get through this situation. Show yourself some compassion. Consider talking to someone you trust about how you are feeling. Whatever it is that helps you empower yourself in a positive way, that is a good thing for you to do.

Feelings Of Failure And Guilt

The human body is amazing. Through my diagnosis of infertility and IVF treatment cycles, we were given a glimpse into an intricate inner world. We saw our babies as five-day-old blastocysts – their embryonic journey hadn't even begun yet. Likewise, through the medical technology of ultrasonography, we saw our babies at different stages of their embryonic and foetal journeys and that was equally mind-blowingly amazing. It is a marvellous and wonderfully complex inner world where the journey of life begins for each of us. However, when something goes horribly wrong with the pregnancy, we gain a new level of awareness and we may even feel that our body has let us down. We may experience deep feelings of failure.

When I see a pregnant woman, I think of her unborn baby – safe and protected. I think this is why people feel such intense guilt when a baby dies during the pregnancy. And when an unborn baby dies, the resultant grief leaves many unanswered questions.

Grieving parents may feel personal responsibility for the loss, including feeling guilty for not being able to protect their unborn child. They may even feel guilty for not realising their baby had died. They are likely to ask, "Was it something I did – or didn't – do?" These feelings of guilt can persist even when parents know there was nothing they could have done to change the outcome. Because the truth is: if they could have, they would have.

Feeling that you have somehow failed your baby twin who died can be overwhelming for parents and it is hard work emotionally to not give in to self-blame. This is when parents have to be kind to themselves and to each other. "Why did our baby have to die?" is a haunting question and it may always remain unanswered.

Somehow, some way, you have to find a way to be at peace, with or without answers. Again, this is all a part of working through grief and coming to a place of accepting that it wasn't your fault, that your baby twin died and there was nothing you could have done to prevent it. When you, as grieving parents, take on the blame of something of this magnitude, then your challenge becomes to show some self-compassion. Hear me when I say: it wasn't your fault. You need to be gentle and kind to yourselves, and to be understanding because you did the best you could.

Feeling Helpless And Vulnerable

The waves of grief can catch you unawares and, at times, they can be disempowering. In those early days of grief, those waves will threaten to knock you off your feet. There is an overwhelming sense that everything that happens is outside of your control. This may be, for the first time as an adult, that you have felt so emotionally vulnerable and it is a very uncomfortable feeling. It may not be an easy thing for you to trust your emotions with others, allowing them to look after you.

Allow your loss to show you the resilience and strength that you possess within. Take it one day at a time and you will regain your sense of self and autonomy in life. It is not going to feel like this forever.

Feeling Isolated

Grieving can leave you feeling isolated from family and friends who don't understand the depth of your loss and grief. This is especially true of multiple birth bereavement because grief isn't what we first think of when we see a mother cradling a baby in her arms. Some people just won't "get it", whilst others will want to reach out to you, but will be unsure of how and when. They may wait until they see an indication from you that you are "ready" for contact with the outside world again.

Now more than ever, you need to feel understood, accepted and supported through your grief. Having good networks of both social and peer support will help facilitate that. Yet, sometimes, in order to elicit the emotional care we need as bereaved parents, we must educate those around us about what we are going through and articulate what our needs are. In the midst of a time filled with emotional turmoil and exhaustion, it should not be this way… but it often is. I like to think of it in this way: As complex as the grieving process is, the needs of the bereaved are often very simple – to be heard, to feel understood, to be validated and to feel empowered.

Maintaining a sense of normality in your everyday life will help lessen those feelings of isolation. For example, arranging a coffee date with a friend or family member can get you out of the house, even if for just an hour or so. Sometimes a change of scenery can make a huge difference. It does help to balance our need to grieve with a sense of normality.

Feeling Misunderstood

You feel totally overwhelmed because you are attending to the needs of a baby who depends on you for everything. This is something that every new parent will appreciate because it is all-consuming and emotionally exhausting! You are thankful to have your surviving twin in your arms and, of course, everyone around you adores him/her. Thankfully, most people will understand that those early weeks and months with a newborn are exhausting.

What they may not appreciate though, is that running parallel to those joys of parenting your newborn twin, is the overwhelming grief you have for your baby twin who has died. They may even look at your grief and misinterpret it as you not coping with the demands of parenthood. I think that's where a comment like "How would you have coped with two babies?" comes from.

However, coping with acute grief on top of looking after the needs of a newborn baby is an entirely different circumstance to being tired (understandably!) from looking after the needs of two babies. This misinterpretation stems from a lack of understanding of what you have been through. If people are able to think more empathically about your situation, then they will likely have a better understanding of what you might need.

As we discussed previously, your emotional connection with both babies runs very deep. And yet, whilst you already have a strong emotional bond with both of your babies, your family and friends are developing a relationship with your surviving twin. The emotional connection they have with your baby twin who has died will be different from yours. This is why the funeral is a significant event and an important opportunity for family and friends to gather around their loved ones and support them as they grieve such a profound loss. It is also perhaps the only opportunity many in your various social circles will have to make an emotional connection with your baby twin who has died.

Just as you will no doubt talk about the beautiful baby you hold in your arms, you need that same freedom to talk about both of your twins. You need to know that when you say his/her name, it will be accepted. It is so important to be heard and understood, to feel emotionally safe and supported as you talk about and express the feelings associated with your loss, taking the time you need to grieve in a way that feels natural for you.

Feeling Pressured

With the whole experience of grief being so intense, it can realistically take a few years to work through it all. It takes time to find healthy ways of coping. Grief is not a negative emotion and it is not something you should be expected to "get over". You shouldn't have to "put on a brave face" just to make others feel comfortable spending time with you. Those around you should recognise your grief as the way in which you express your love for your baby twin. They also need to understand that you will likely always have these same feelings of love and sadness when you think about him/her. And that's okay.

With grief being such a personal process that we go through, it is true to say that whilst you and your partner are both grieving the loss of your baby twin, you will both likely grieve in different ways. Just as our life experiences and way of viewing the world are individual, so too can be the ways in which we grieve. It helps to understand and to respect the differences in how each partner grieves and to offer each individual the support they need.

One partner may seek out others who have had a similar experience of loss — joining support groups, openly expressing feelings and identifying with others for emotional support. Other partners may seek out solitude or the company of one or two trusted friends. They may express their grief in a physical way, such as through exercise or sport. Remember, you are in this together as a couple and you need to support one another as you grieve on a deeply personal level. There is no right or wrong way to grieve. There is also no timeline for grief. Grief is an intuitive, instinctive process and we need to express our grief in a way that feels natural, individual and personal.

Feeling Violated

Death can also make you feel violated in a few different ways. In this case, like a thief in the night, death has robbed you of something so precious. Death leaves behind only the memories, unfulfilled dreams and a precious few mementos of your baby's existence. Having to pack up your baby's belongings and finalise their life can add to the feeling of being robbed. It is hard to understand and accept why someone so precious – so loved and wanted – has been taken away from you. You were already saying good-bye before you'd even had a chance to properly say hello.

Also, in a very real sense, grief takes you away from you. On the one hand, there is your non-grieving self, your innocent self before loss, and that's the part of you that you have lost and you miss. On the other hand, there is your grieving self, and it may seem as if you are oscillating between being very emotionally regressed or as an emotionally exaggerated version of yourself. There may be days when you barely recognise the face that looks back at you in the mirror. You're still you but you've lost a part of yourself.

Just as I can look back to the day of my mid-pregnancy ultrasound and say that was the day my life changed forever, you will always be able to pinpoint the moment you realised everything had changed forever for you and your twins. As much as you want to return to that safe, happy place from before your loss occurred, you know that there is no going back. This leaves you questioning if life will ever return to normal, to the way it was before your loss. In this way, grief is confronting, because a part of you has changed forever and deep down you know that things will never be exactly the same again.

It is okay to grieve that lost part of yourself. The important thing is to take that sense of loss and create something that has meaning for you. There will always be a special place in your heart for your baby twin who has died, where they will forever remain as you move forward with your life. Life will take on a new sense of normal and, even though it may not feel like it now, you will find joy again. You will find that whilst some things have changed forever, other things will always remain the same. You will look at life and love and loss through different eyes and with a deeper understanding of what a precious gift life is. Your baby twin may not be with you in the physical sense, but he/she lives on in your heart and nothing can ever take that away from you.

Feeling Anger And Frustration

I think any of the preceding feelings can contribute to feelings of frustration and anger. There is an overwhelming sense that, in a perfect world, things would have been very different. From a grieving parents' point of view, the death of a baby is intensely unfair and senseless. Anger is an understandable and natural response to such deep emotional pain. As it is a powerful emotion, it is important to find ways of expressing it, both emotionally and physically, in a safe and healthy way. Somehow, as grieving parents, you have to find a way to be at peace with the unfairness and senselessness of your baby's death.

In the context of a multiple pregnancy, grieving parents also have to find a way to be at peace with their surviving baby growing up without their twin by their side. An important element of this is trying to help others understand all that this means not just to you as parents, but also in the future, what is means to your surviving twin.

Your Grief Will Always Be There

To work through this maze of feelings is to experience the pain of your grief. When you think of grief in the context of love, the grief doesn't ever need to leave you. However, the intensity of these feelings – as overwhelming as they are in acute grief – will lessen as you work through them. I daresay never a day will pass when you don't think about your baby twin who has died and those thoughts will always be tinged with sadness. That is the nature of grief. Ongoing grief is actually a beautiful expression of love and it allows you to remain emotionally connected to your baby twin. You will know that you have grieved well when, in remembering your baby, you find that the intense pain has lessened and some peace has entered into your heart.

You will find, through the years, that your grief will resurface from time-to-time. It may be specific times of the year like your twins' birthday and other special dates, or it may be something else that reminds you of your baby twin. It may be a significant event in your family or a special milestone that your surviving twin reaches. Grief can resurface for any number of reasons, but when it does you will once again you find yourself swimming across the river of your grief. The difference is, each time you navigate your way through those waters, you will find a new strength and renewed confidence that you will cope again – because you have in the past.

Unresolved Grief

I will close this chapter with a reminder that going through grief is necessary. It is unhealthy not to allow your grief to be felt. Trying to contain such deep emotions, rather than express them, is not helpful to you (and everyone around you) in the long-term. You can't ignore grief and it will not go away of its own accord. Eventually, unexpressed and unresolved grief will re-emerge somewhere down the track, demanding your attention. It will express itself in other, less healthy ways such as an ongoing, unresolved anger, the recurrence of prior mental illness or development of a reliance on prescribed or illicit drugs and/or alcohol use. These things will only serve to complicate and prolong your grieving process. It is, therefore, far better in the long-term to express your grief in a way that comes naturally to you (as painful as that is). Of course, talking to your GP about eliciting professional supports is well worth considering. In chapter three, we will look at the various supports that are available and I would encourage you to link into the social, peer and professional supports around you rather than trying to deal with the intensity of your grief on your own.

Chapter Three

You Are Not Alone

From my poetry collection © 2015

Dear Younger Me,
Let go of the situations
that you can't control or change.
Let go of the hurt of feeling misunderstood.
Life is too short to worry about these things.
It is also too long.
Embrace the situations
you can control and change.
Do it to create a positive
and meaningful world around you.
Embrace the friends
who wish to connect with you.
Allow them in to accept you, love you
and understand you.
As they have been your soft place to fall,
be theirs in return.
Nurture those friendships,
cherish them, enjoy them.
Love them like family.
Keep looking for the positives in life.
Never give up on what you believe in.
With love,
The Older Me
who has walked a mile in your shoes.

Standing on the kerb in the rain, the police officer and I surveyed the damage to my car. It was still drivable. The main thing on my mind at that particular moment was: it got me here and, he assured me, it would get me home.

Realising I had driven up from the South Coast that morning, he asked what I was doing in North Sydney.

I replied that I had been invited as one of several guest speakers at a conference for health care professionals on managing multiple births. I explained that I had been invited to share my experience of when things go wrong in a twin pregnancy with one of the babies dying before birth, adding that I considered this opportunity a privilege.

Pondering on that for a moment, the police officer responded with, "Well, that would be information you would know on a need-to-know basis only."

With those words he acknowledged that multiple birth bereavement is a little-known area of grief and loss. His take on it highlighted to me that there is such a huge deficit of knowledge about the emotional impact of multiple birth bereavement and subsequent to this, of readily available, appropriate support. I couldn't help but also think that this is how grieving bereaved parents can so easily become disenfranchised.

Our Need for People to Gather Around Us

In chapter one, we looked at the immediate needs that grieving parents may have as they mentally prepare themselves for the births of their twins. As the news of your loss spreads through your social circles, family and friends may reach out offering their support. This might take the form of help around the house or offering to look after your older children. It may be giving you the opportunity to rest for a few hours. Whether you are still awaiting the birth of your babies or are establishing a routine of sorts with your newborn surviving twin, think of ways that your extended circles of family and friends can offer you practical assistance with minimal interruption to your normal household routine.

Support comes in many forms. It could be the simple act of someone making you a cup of coffee or cooking a family meal. It could be running a few loads of washing through the machine and hanging them on the clothesline, folding clean washing or stacking the dishwasher. It could be sitting with your older children and reading them a book, playing a board game with them or going for a walk. It can occur in a chance encounter with an old friend in the supermarket aisle or through the ongoing nurture of long-term friendships. It may be a card or handwritten note that arrives in the letterbox just to let you know you are being thought of. When the support is there, it can make a huge difference.

Yet, it needs to be understood that some days you may need some time and space for yourself and that is okay. It is helpful for things to be planned with others in advance, so long as it is also understood that following a rough night with an unsettled baby or when you simply need some me-time, those plans may have to be postponed.

Trust Your Gut Feeling

Grief and trauma expose us at our best and at our worst – they also expose others at their best and at their worst. Those around us will likely really struggle to grasp the emotional impact of what we have been through and subsequently, they will struggle to know what to say to us. I think it is really important that we trust our gut feelings about people and the different situations we will encounter as we go about our day-to-day life.

In the same way that some people will make us feel very safe with them emotionally – and we know that whatever we disclose to them will be understood in context and respected – that same emotional safety won't be there for us with other people. Whilst they may be well-meaning, some people may blurt their words out because they don't know what else to say. You may feel their words are hurtful, however, they may not even realise that what they said is upsetting to you (they may not even be able to recall later exactly what they said). The impact of their words on you may also depend on how important that relationship is to you. It does make it easier to forgive someone if they realise their words were hurtful, however, they may not ever realise and that leaves you with having to find a way to forgive them anyway. In forgiving them, you do so to free yourself from the hurt. Remember, just as this is uncharted territory for you, it is likewise also for them. It may help you to consider that they are likely really struggling to understand your situation.

Other people may simply be curious about your loss and whilst they too are well-meaning, they may ask questions that make you feel uncomfortable. "How many children do you have?" is perhaps the one question that every bereaved parent will struggle with at some point or another. It is important not to feel pressured into talking about your loss, just because someone has asked. We have our gut feelings for a reason and we need to learn to listen to them. If we don't feel emotionally safe with a person, then it's okay to not say too much. Some people will understand and respect that you are (and always will be) the parents of twins – and thank goodness for those people! They are the people we need in our circles of support.

Personally, I have found that my answers to those tricky questions people ask are situation-specific and my answers depend on who I am talking to and how I feel about them and the conversation. There is, however, no right or wrong way for you to approach this. It really does depend on what feels right for you in that moment. The idiom "don't throw your pearl to the swine" comes to mind because not everyone will try to understand your situation of loss or be kind with their words. We all have long-held beliefs and when it comes to things like pregnancy loss, some people will draw on their beliefs, often without choosing their words carefully or considering the impact their words will have on you. They will default to saying things such as: "It wasn't a baby anyway... Miscarriage is nature's way of getting rid of her mistakes... You can always have another baby... (and my personal favourite) Be happy you have one baby!" I speak from experience when I say it's not worth having to deal with the ignorance of some people. Yet, it saddens me that some people think it's okay to argue the point over our baby twin's humanity and dismiss our loss. It is better to walk away from those conversations with your head held high. This all goes back to allowing your gut feeling about a person to guide you as you respond to their questions and their curiosity. In a very real sense, you are protecting the memory of your baby twin.

Feeling Safe Emotionally

Feeling emotional safety is imperative when talking to anyone about your loss. You need to know that that person will be there as your soft place to fall, if that's what you need them to be. Having emotional safety allows you to be vulnerable and that vulnerability allows you to elicit the nurture and care that you need.

It is also important that you feel secure in the knowledge that whatever you say to a trusted friend or relative will be understood in context and that the confidentiality of what you say will be respected. This is important because of that vulnerability you are already feeling. It is entirely up to you who to trust with your thoughts and feelings, and again, having that emotional safety with a person will be a good indication of that for you.

When we feel emotionally safe with another person, we will talk… and we will likely also cry. It may be something we suddenly remember or something someone says to us, but in that moment just what we need to do is to cry, to really cry - to cry for as long as we need and to stop when we feel we are ready. When we cry, our body releases the endorphin oxytocin, which helps bring some relief to our emotional pain. This helps explain the importance of being "allowed" to cry rather than having someone soothe our tears away before we are ready.

Helplines

It may be reassuring to know that there are a few helplines you can reach out to any time you feel you'd like to talk to someone. This is especially true if you find nights the hardest, when it seems everyone is asleep except for you. It might make the world of difference to you to talk to someone in the here-and-now, not putting it off until "tomorrow".

Though you won't know the person you are talking to, they will have an understanding of what you are going through and of what you might need in that moment.

Below are a few National Helplines in Australia which offer phone counselling for grieving families as well as anyone in a supportive role – family, friends and health care professionals.

PANDA (Perinatal Anxiety and Depression Australia)

PANDA is a specialist perinatal mental health helpline, offering support to expectant and new parents and their health care providers. The PANDA Helpline is open daytime and evenings, Monday to Saturday.

Phone: 1300 726 306

Website: https://panda.org.au

Red Nose Australia (including SANDS)

Red Nose Australia, which SANDS became a part of in 2020, provides bereavement support to families and friends affected by the loss of a pregnancy or the death of a baby or child. Their 24/7 support line is answered by a team who are specially trained in supporting families who have experienced child loss.

Phone: 1300 308 307

Website: https://www.sands.org.au

Lifeline Australia

You can talk to Lifeline Australia at any time of the day or night. Lifeline also offers a crisis online chat. The Lifeline call-takers are trained to talk about a wide range of crises that their callers may be experiencing – again, it might be reassuring just to know they are there.

Phone: 13 11 14
Website: https://www.lifeline.org.au/

Mensline Australia

Mensline Australia offers a phone and online counselling service at any time of the day or night. Their aim is to provide support to men Australia-wide.

Phone: 1300 78 99 78.
Website: https://mensline.org.au/phone-and-online-counselling/

13YARN

13YARN offers 24/7 phone counselling for Aboriginal and Torres Strait Islander Australians. If you are feeling worried or no good, then the 13YARN crisis telephone supporter will be there for you.

Phone: 13 92 76
Website: https://www.13yarn.org.au/

Kids Helpline Australia

Offering phone and web-chat counselling, the Kids Helpline Australia is specifically for children aged 5 to 12, teens aged 13 to 17 and young adults aged 18 to 25.

Phone: 1800 55 1800
Website: https://kidshelpline.com.au/

Professional Supports

As we saw in chapter two, the grieving process arising from multiple birth bereavement is complicated and the impact on the mental well-being of grieving parents can be quite profound. Most people don't know what you are going through or what you will need from them in terms of support. This makes it all the more important to have appropriate support around you. Feeling well-supported is an important part of grieving and healing. It is also an important part of our ongoing mental and emotional well-being.

As we talked about in chapter one, if ever you feel overwhelmed and way out of your depth with your grief, then seeking out professional supports is worth considering. However, it can be overwhelming knowing where to look for an appropriate grief counsellor locally. Talking to your GP about a mental health plan and referral is a good place to start. (If you have had a pre-existing history of depression or other mental illness then you may already be under the care of a psychologist.)

Having the support of a counsellor or psychologist can make the world of difference as you work through specific areas with which you are struggling. The death of your baby has resulted in you navigating your way through an unknown world and you shouldn't have to go it alone. At first, it may feel strange to talk to someone you have only just met about the most traumatic event you have experienced, but with time and care the therapeutic relationship should be of great benefit to you. Just to have a supportive person who gives you the time and space you need to talk about the trauma and helps you seek to make sense of it all can make a huge difference to the way in which you grieve. In the long-term, your mental and emotional well-being will benefit greatly from it too.

Peer Support

Still fresh in our memories is March 2020, when much of the world's population was in lock-down due to the COVID-19 pandemic. I couldn't help but notice that during those early days of lock-down, when we were all separated, we felt a heightened need to remain emotionally connected with others. At that time, videos started circulating online of apartment blocks in Italy where the residents all came onto their balconies to sing together. Tenor and baritone voices rang through the air, penetrating the eerie silence. Others joined in, from the safety of their own balconies, with musical instruments or saucepan lids. They were alone, but together. There was a real sense of connectedness. In doing so, these people created something beautiful and meaningful out of what were otherwise very long and lonely days. If there is anything positive to have come out of the COVID-19 pandemic, then it is this heightened awareness of how important it is to manage our mental health and the need to take simple measures to remain emotionally connected with others.

This is a good analogy for grief and loss, and the subsequent need for maintaining our emotional connection with those around us. Grief and trauma can leave us feeling very alone in our experience and disconnected from others. On the one hand, we experience grief at a deeply personal and individual level but, on the other hand, it becomes a part of our broader experience with others. A sense of emotional connection can have a positive influence on the way in which we grieve.

When we take a closer look at the social needs arising from grief, we see that people will often seek out others whose experience of loss and grief is similar to their own. There are a few important reasons for this. The need to be understood is very strong and bereaved people have a very deep need for their loss to be validated by others. They need to feel that the depth of their grief has been understood. This is especially true if they already feel disenfranchised by others in their loss. However, it may be challenging to find others with whom to connect - others who have also experienced multiple birth bereavement.

The lingering sense that what I had experienced with my own twin pregnancy was quite rare served to strengthen my resolve to connect with other twin mums like me. My early searches for anything twin-loss related locally all took me to our local Multiple Birth Club. I did attend a few club meetings but, despite their warm welcome, I felt very much the odd one out. They didn't seem to cater much for twin mums like me. Personally, in the early days of my own loss, I also found it quite confronting to see intact sets of multiple birth children – it was a visual reminder of how dramatically my life had changed.

I also met with a small group of parents who had all had "singleton" pregnancies resulting in miscarriage, stillbirth and neonatal death. We had all experienced the trauma of loss and were united in our grief. However, with my young surviving twin in my arms, I felt the odd one out here too, keenly aware that those courageous parents all left the hospital with empty arms. These realisations intensified my yearning for contact with others who, through their own lived experiences, understood the complexities of what I had been through.

My experience of peer support specifically for twin loss goes back as far as 2001. When my surviving twin was five months old, I came into contact with a woman in outback Western Australia, whose infant twin had died just a few months before my twins were born. As we were not aware of any other support group in

Australia specifically for multiple birth bereavement, I thought it timely to form an online peer support group specifically for twin loss, which I named OzMOST – an acronym for "Aussie Mums of Surviving Twins". The group was created as a safe haven for parents all over Australia, raising their surviving child of a multiple pregnancy.

Whilst we each go through our own personal experience of grief and loss, through peer support there is a sense of connectedness, of being in it together – not unlike those Italian residents on their balconies! Each member's circumstance of twin loss is individual and unique, but there are also experiences and feelings that we all have in common. For some members, their baby twin died during the pregnancy or at birth, others had their baby twin die in the days or weeks following the birth. For some the experience is recent, for others it may be a number of years ago. Some were able to see and hold their babies, others weren't. Some were able to say goodbye to their babies, others weren't. All of us have felt misunderstood because we still had a living baby to care for. No matter where we each are in our journey of grief, the group is there to offer emotional support to one another.

Peer support can play an important role in a bereaved person's journey through their grief, because the understanding amongst peers often goes beyond empathy – they understand because of their common lived experience and that is a very powerful dynamic which can be very helpful and healing. It is because of this unique bond and understanding that members can find the encouragement that they need to grieve their loss – something that is hard to do when you still have a living child (or children) to take care of. What is important here is to connect with others who "get it" about the significance of the loss.

Remember, bereaved parents are grieving for many things:

- The loss of their child and their imagined future before their child died.
- Their loss of their status as parents of this child and, importantly, as the parents of twins.
- Their sense of self: the nature of grief is such that loss will often leave us asking, "Who am I now?"

Through peer support, grieving parents can work through these issues together. The beauty of peer support is that it is reciprocal – you give support to other members in order to receive some support in return. It helps normalise the experience of loss for everyone concerned. Whilst individuals will journey together in their grief (and often, in doing so, form lifelong friendships), they can also give hope to others whose loss is more recent. They can let these parents know that grief is survivable and that it won't always hurt as much as it does in those first few years when the grief is acute.

How We Feel about the Support Around Us

Following a traumatic experience, the way in which you grieve will be influenced by the degree to which you feel supported. This is a time when you have a heightened need to feel understood. You need to know that those around you understand the impact the trauma has had on your emotional well-being as well as your day-to-day functioning. It is not easy working your way through acute grief – feeling well supported by others allows you to work through it at your own pace and in a way that feels natural and congruent for you. It is my sincere hope that you will be able to say that, for the most part, you have felt supported by those who have gathered around you.

Thankfully, as we have seen in this chapter, support can come from our own circles of family and friends as they gather around us, offering help in practical ways around the house as well as providing emotional support. People harness their nervous energy from wanting to help and at such times, you will see the kindness that they extend to you and you will be humbled by their generosity. Accept it knowing that if the situations were reversed, you would do the same for them.

At other times, eliciting some emotional support for ourselves may require us to reach out to a helpline or to seek out a counsellor or psychologist for professional support. Or we may gain support through connecting with others whose experience of loss is similar to ours. It does take a lot of courage to reach out and it may take you several weeks (or even months) to feel ready to take that big, brave step. You will know when it is the right time for you to do that.

The Flip Side

There is a flip side to this as well. You may need to take a step back from some people. It may be that someone in your extended circle of family or friends has a child of the same age and gender as your baby twin who has died. As much as you have valued your relationship with them up until this point, for now it hurts too much to be around them. I hope that one day, you will find your way back to those people and that in the meantime, you will allow your broken heart to heal.

Some grieving parents may find that during this time, when they need people to gather around them, not everyone will be there to offer support. Some people won't be able to provide you with the emotional support you need. Some will just quietly respect your situation but not necessarily communicate that to you. Others may not recognise your baby twin's humanity or acknowledge your loss. Some people may deliberately avoid you. Some friendships may even fall by the wayside. I think for the most part, people are well-meaning but many don't know how to handle our situation. Our loss and grief makes them feel uncomfortable, and for that reason, it's easier for them to stay away. To try and keep these people in your circles of support will add a burden of unnecessary grief for you to bear.

I have always believed that when one door closes in our life, another door opens. Whilst I often think of this in the context of opportunities, I think it is equally applicable to the relationships that come and go in our life. I think it is also true to say that as some relationships and friendships may fade away, our loss will bring other people into our life, people with whom we may not have otherwise crossed paths, and beautiful friendships can grow from there. I've heard it said many times that it is through the really difficult situations we encounter in life, that we learn what is important and who our true friends are. Loss brings many changes into our lives – it changes us and how we view the world. It's entirely up to us to create something meaningful out of it all.

Chapter Four

Grief is Survivable

From my poetry collection © 2015

Dear Younger Me,
I won't lie to you –
the emotional process of grief is hard work,
especially early on.
You will have days when you feel
completely overwhelmed and alone.
There will be times when those around you
resist the process you have to go through.
I want you to know that you will withstand
those darker days and the pressure to "get over it"
as though "it" was a head cold or stomach bug.
You will learn the value of living life
just one day at a time.
This is one of the greatest lessons of grief.
You will appreciate just being in the moment
and you will view life and love and relationships
and loss through different eyes.
Though you can't imagine life without Meggie just yet,
there will come a day when you will know
she has her own special place in your heart.
There she will stay forevermore.
Safe, right where her little heart once beat under yours –
never to be taken away again.
And on that day, peace will enter in.
You will more fully understand
that not even death can break the bond of love.
With love,
The Older Me,
who has walked a mile in your shoes.

A Year of Firsts

The year following a loss is filled with many firsts. As grieving parents, this is especially true as you watch your surviving twin grow and develop. Your surviving twin will experience all those special firsts in life that make your heart sing – their first smile, their first giggle, their first word, their first step. These are sweet little milestones that bring joy. There will be other "firsts" to experience as well and those occasions may feel more bittersweet, especially in the days leading up to them. Significant days like your twins' birthday, Mothers' Day, Fathers' Day, Christmas, Easter and any other day when we gather together to celebrate and enjoy an occasion.

There will be some days that you will always associate with the death of your baby twin, such as the anniversary of their death, and it is as equally hard to avoid those days as it is to go through them. With the coming and going of such significant days, there will be other good-byes that you will have to say to your baby twin. Each passing year can feel like a lifetime, on the one hand, but just like yesterday on the other. As you slowly adjust to your "new normal", you will learn to do what feels right for you and your household. Just as you have been grieving in a way that is natural to you, you will need to use that same intuition for those significant days. This is especially true for your twins' birthday and the anniversary of your baby twin's death.

Another "first" that you will encounter, sooner or later, is your surviving twin's awareness of themselves as a twin, or perhaps more accurately, as a twinless-twin. The kind and gentle approach is to nurture your surviving twin in their own self-awareness and work with what they already know in an age-appropriate way. They will take their cues from you. It is so important to convey to them that they, as your surviving twin child, are so loved and wanted for the beautiful, unique person they are – that nobody could ever take their place and that they won't be living their life in the shadow of their twin sibling. Your surviving twin may take it all in his/her stride at some times and then struggle with it at other times. Just as you and your partner need support and understanding through your own grief, your surviving twin may as well. At some point down the track, eliciting professional support through a grief counsellor who works with children may be worthwhile considering.

Your Grief Won't Always Be This Raw
Grief has a way of completely knocking the stuffing out of you. There are those days when your entire world stops and you wonder how everyone around you can continue on "as normal". But then there comes a day when you realise that despite the overwhelming sense of loss, despite the feeling that your heart has broken in two, despite the feeling that everything has changed forever (because it has)… despite all of this, your heart still beats. You start to realise your own inner strength, your resilience, your courage. And bravely, you forge ahead, one step at a time. The first year or two following a loss are the hardest to get through. You know at one level you will get through this, but at so many other levels, you may question how? And you may wonder who will you be when you get there?

While I was still in the maternity ward with my newborn twin, the hospital social worker gave me the name and number of a woman who, some years prior, had also experienced the death of her infant twin. It took me six months to pluck up the courage to dial her number. We arranged to meet together in the northern suburbs, with a small group of other twin loss mums.

In those early months, I put my grieving on hold but now I felt more ready to elicit some support for myself. The women were all lovely and welcomed me with open arms, and they made a big fuss over my very cute six-month-old surviving twin. The view from the front room was of the ocean and we saw a few whales making their annual migration along the coastline. It was a beautiful sight to see. Normally, I would have been just as excited to see the whales as they all were, but it was very early days for me and I was still processing the emotional trauma of my pregnancy and the birth. As this was my first opportunity to meet face-to-face with other twin mums like me, I needed to talk about what I had been through in the last year or so. I really needed to know they "got me". Unfortunately, the opportunity to talk in depth about our experiences of loss didn't present itself and I went home that day with very mixed feelings. I so desperately needed an emotional bond with other twin mums like me but it was obvious, with migrating whales being their topic of choice, that they were at a very different place in their grief.

Although the meeting didn't go as I had anticipated, there were a few valuable lessons. As I mulled the experience over later I realised, firstly, that grief isn't always going to feel as raw as it does in that first year. Secondly, the experience was a clear demonstration to me that grief is survivable and that, as time goes on, life will take on a new sense of normal. I understood that I was in a very different place to where these women were. I was still just surviving the waves of my own grief, struggling to get through life one day at a time. I hadn't yet considered what life would be like beyond this "new normal".

I have noticed through the years that when people get to a certain place in their grief, they find it difficult to "go back to that place" again. I get it. It's a raw place. It's a place where the sad memories and tears always just bubble under the surface and it takes so much of your energy just to be present and start enjoying life again. Going back there risks you unravelling and having to re-ravel all over again. However, I have also learnt through peer support that it's not necessarily about going back to that raw place again, but rather it is about conveying that you have been there and that you understand how overwhelming that new, raw grief is… but also that you have survived it. That's what I needed to hear from those women that day. That they had been there too.

Keep It Manageable

You may remember in my introduction I posed these two questions, "Just how do you experience joy and sadness simultaneously? And just as perplexing, how do you separate them when the feelings are so overwhelming?" Remember… you are grieving. You have a surviving twin who depends on you for everything. You have a grieving partner. You possibly have older children who are also grieving, yet need and rely on you to maintain their routine and sense of normality. It is important to keep things as manageable as possible. Be kind to yourself. Be kind to your partner. Be patient with one another. Look after each other.

When it comes to your twins' birthday, it might be helpful for you to honour each child on separate days. It may be helpful to celebrate your living twin on one day and honour the memory of your baby twin on another day. If there is a day other than your twins' birthday that you associate with your baby twin who has died, it may help to separate the two dates that way. Examples may include the anniversary of their death, their funeral day, or any other day that has special significance. Just as you would have celebrated your twins in equal measure if they were both in your arms, similarly, it can help to separate the days, so that you have the time and care you need to devote to each child on their own special day.

I am not suggesting that for those special days, that you focus on one twin and forget about the other. You and I both know that that's impossible to do. What I am saying, though, is give yourself some breathing space so that you can honour each child in a meaningful way – celebrating and making happy memories with your surviving twin on their birthday, and giving yourself permission to feel sad and honour your baby twin on their special day.

Self-Care

It is understandable that grief and emotional trauma will have an impact on many areas of our daily functioning. We can experience grief in somatic ways and a loss of appetite or lack of sleep are very common. You may wake feeling exhausted each morning and have very little energy or enthusiasm for the day ahead. As I have said earlier, going through acute grief is, for a time, both exhausting and all-consuming. It slows you down and you may find yourself living life one day at a time, pacing yourself sometimes hour-by-hour or even moment-by-moment when you need to.

On those days, when everything just seems that little bit harder, it may be wise to have a plan to help you get through. Write yourself a list of the things you would like to achieve for the day. Keep it realistic and don't expect too much of yourself. There may just be one thing that you need to focus your attention on in the here-and-now to help get you through. Think about how you are going to get through the next hour. It all goes back to keeping it manageable.

I think, by far, the kindest thing we can do for ourselves is to allow our feelings to come and go. When you feel sad, it's okay to allow those sad feelings. Trying to keep them at bay is like being a juggler who can keep all the balls in the air for a while, but not indefinitely. Sooner or later, one of those balls is going to fall out of rhythm and out of sync with the others. Another way of thinking about this is attempting to hold a beach ball under water. It takes all of your effort but you can only hold the ball under the water for a while before it slips through your fingers and up into the air. Rather than fighting our sad feelings and pushing them deep down, it is much better – and an important part of experiencing grief – to allow them to come and go. Just as surely as you have those sad days where you wake with tears trickling down your cheeks, the happier days will also follow.

In the early days of my grief, I can remember trying to recall the last time I laughed, like really laughed… and then one day when I did laugh, it caught me off guard. The happy, light-hearted days seemed so few and far between in those early days of grief but when they came, they were a much-needed reprieve from the sadness. These days are so good for your soul. Give yourself permission to enjoy those happy light-hearted times. You need them.

Also in those early days of my grief, I kept my feelings very closely guarded. In chapter one, I talked about how some women will use strength as their coping mechanism as they await the births of their twins and this is very true of me and how I coped. Using strength to cope is also part of being an independent person, especially if you are not used to letting people look after your emotional needs. However, grief has a way of making you feel somewhat regressed emotionally. Because I appeared to be strong, I lost count of the times people commended me for coping so well. Yet, I really didn't feel it, and they couldn't see the reality. I honestly didn't know what other choice I had at the time. I was navigating my way through uncharted territory and was just doing the best I could with the information that was made available to me at the time.

I also worried about how my grief was impacting my surviving twin. In a very real sense, he was just as much a part of my survival as I was to his. For the second-half of my twin pregnancy, I often paced myself day-by-day, hour-by-hour and I worked hard at remaining positive and hopeful. After the birth of my twins, he was my reason for getting out of bed every day (and through the night!). He was my reason for maintaining contact with the outside world. He was my hope that we would settle into a good routine of sorts and that, one day, life would take on a new sense of normal. And it did… eventually!

It is also very true to say that taking care of my surviving twin meant that I also had to take care of myself. Through the years I have learnt the value of self-care and of having a written self-care plan. It helps to identify what your needs are and how they can be met. I have found it helpful to look at my needs in the following four categories: mental, physical, social and spiritual. Let's look at each one and see how they might be relevant to where you're at with your own grief and loss.

Just as we did in chapter two, as you look through the following pages, consider:

- What are your specific needs for self-care and how can they be met?
- What has been helpful for you in the past? Is this a good starting point for attending to your self-care needs now?

Mental Well-Being

Looking back to those early years, a lot of my time and effort went into self-preservation. I was acutely aware that the people around me had no knowledge or experience of twin loss during pregnancy or of the subsequent grieving process I would go through. Oftentimes people were too quick to shut down conversations about my experience and so I built up an armour of self-protection to help me get through situations that were unavoidable. This was just another way that meant I came across as strong and coping well. I sensed judgement from those around me for grieving when I had my beautiful, active and mischievous surviving twin to look after. Yes, he brought so much joy and laughter into my life; however, I still had an overwhelming – and largely unmet – need to talk about my experience of loss.

In terms of mental well-being, it may help you to balance out the busy-ness of life with your surviving twin by ensuring some "me-time" for yourself every day. In the busy, daily routine of being a mum, who we are and what our needs are can tend to take a back seat. Your life as it is now may be completely different to what it was pre-pregnancy. You may have been very independent and self-reliant. You may even have gone from a busy and responsible full-time job to being at home with this beautiful, but demanding, little human. Now I know those early days with a young baby are full-on and during the little time you have to yourself, you can feel absolutely exhausted. However, there may come a day when you find you have the energy for something more. When this happens it will help to keep your mind alert and stimulated by doing something that is fun and stress-free, whatever that may be.

It may help to factor in daily sunshine and fresh air, because these are good for our mental health as they increase our levels of the endorphin serotonin (a deficiency of which lends itself to feelings of anxiety and depression). Listen to music that you enjoy. Write something in your journal. Now might be a good time to read that book that has been gathering dust on the coffee table. There is great catharsis in giving your brain a little break from the intensity of your grief.

Giving yourself a break may also mean just having some time to sit and be alone with your thoughts. At these times, it may help to focus on doing something very specific, even if for just a few minutes. It may be something as simple as doing your Kegel pelvic floor exercises. I know it sounds too simple but it also helps to just breathe! The controlled breathing technique taught in the antenatal classes can help keep you calm and feeling more in control, just as much as it helps with the physical pain of labour. Another good way of focusing on your breathing is to learn a few simple Tai Chi exercises. It may also help to do the 5-4-3-2-1 sensory exercise, just to ground you in the moment: name five things you can see, four things you can touch, three things you can hear, two things you can smell and one thing you can taste.

Adult colouring-in books are also quite therapeutic. It is very calming, allowing your thoughts to wander as the lines and shapes on the page come to life with colour. Having that time and space to think and "be" is sometimes just what we need to calm our minds and feel relaxed. This is also a really good way to unravel our thoughts and work things out.

In chapter three, we talked about how grieving parents will often seek out others whose experience of loss and grief is similar to their own. As well as seeking peer support, another way to do this is to read articles and books on loss and grief. The beauty of this approach is that you often get to see another person's story in its entirety – this will give you a sense of what their life was like before their loss occurred, together with their experience of the loss itself and their grief as they adjusted to life without their loved one. Reading about other people's life experiences can help lessen the feelings of isolation that we often feel in grief and provide reassurance that what we are going through is very understandable and that grief is survivable.

Physical Well-Being

As hard as it is when you are feeling exhausted and emotionally drained on some days, it is important to look after your physical well-being. The obvious things include maintaining a sensible and balanced eating plan, ensuring you get enough sleep (although I do know how much of a challenge that is when you are attending to your baby through the night!) and doing some physical activity each day. Bundling up your surviving twin in the pram to go for a walk around the block or to have a play at the local park is also a good way to factor in some fresh air and sunshine. Besides, the sun's warm rays on your skin can make you feel good and happy. Again, as obvious as it sounds, drinking water is also important. When we become anxious our thirst increases, so it makes good sense to keep well hydrated.

It may also be helpful to book yourself in for a neck and shoulder massage. Skin-on-skin contact can be very soothing. With a sensitive and thoughtful massage therapist, this can become a time when someone attends to your needs. It is easy to neglect ourselves when we are grieving and looking after everyone else, so having a little nurture for ourselves can be a very powerful and emotional experience in grief. Many years ago I had the most wonderful masseuse. She was studying towards qualifications in an entirely different profession, but I was a regular client while she was still taking appointments for massages. She understood my need for silence and, with the exception of ambient music playing softly in the background, she respected that. She also understood that at some point during the session, I might cry and that that was okay. The hour with her was my time for self-care and she was so very caring and nurturing.

Sexual intimacy may also be an important part of grieving and healing together for both partners. Sometimes grief brings couples together sexually, sometimes it takes a while to resume sexual intimacy. There is no right or wrong, there is just whatever is best for both of you. Emotional trauma can also have an impact on sexual functioning for both men and women (it doesn't discriminate), and this too can take time and care to return to a sense of normality again. However, if this is an ongoing area of concern for yourself or your partner, then it may be helpful to talk to a counsellor who specialises in sex therapy.

Social Needs

It's a basic human need to feel emotionally connected to others. As time goes by, and perhaps with many people thinking you're over the worst of it now, maintaining those emotional connections may become all the more important. When we are in acute grief it can be tricky navigating some relationships. Many people in our wider social circles will take a step back, allowing us the time and space we need in those early weeks and months. Perhaps they are also waiting for us to make that first move – to let them know that we are ready. It may take a while before we are ready to have contact with those wider social circles again and that's okay.

In chapter three we talked about our need to feel emotionally safe when we are talking to others about our experience of grief. It is good to spend quality time with the people who make us feel safe. It takes a lot of effort and courage to take those first steps towards normality again and having the support of close, trusted friends who create that "safe place" can help us heal little-by-little. It also helps to enjoy the friendships for what they are and to allow those light-hearted moments that make us laugh back into our lives again.

Spiritual Connection

In this context I talk about spirituality as the personal practice of cultivating a sense of peace and meaning when thinking about your baby twin who has died. I think in terms of self-care, the question is: what do you need to do to get to that place of peace and meaning? This may mean working your way through a maze of feelings and the subsequent emotional and cognitive needs as discussed in chapter two. It may mean forgiving yourself for not realising something was wrong until it was too late. It may mean being kind to yourself for being in a situation way beyond your ability to control. It may mean coming to a place of acceptance that there will always be some questions to which there will never be an answer. This is the hard work of grief, working through the really tough questions, knowing that there may not be answers but that you somehow, some way, need to be at peace with them. Whatever it is that allows some more peace to enter into your heart, that's what you need to do.

As always, I strongly believe in putting professional supports in place when we feel out of our depth and it may be helpful to talk these things through with a grief counsellor or psychologist. You may find great catharsis in hearing yourself say your thoughts out loud as you seek to make sense of it all in the context of a safe, supportive place, especially with someone who is familiar with talking about emotional trauma and grief-related issues. Eliciting some professional support for yourself in this way can help provide you with the knowledge you need to grieve in a way that is both natural to you and good for your mental well-being.

Nobody knows you – and what you need – in quite the way that you do and that makes self-care all the more important. Being self-aware and being diligent about looking after every aspect of our lives is empowering. It is good to know that there is something we do have control over, especially with the appropriate supports in place. Good self-care also means that you will be able to find so much more joy in parenting your surviving twin and enjoying your time with them for the beautiful, unique child that they are.

Memorialising

Memory Box

Memorialising your baby twin who has died means creating a meaningful way to remain emotionally connected to them. It means your baby twin will always retain their status within your family, even though the expression of that relationship has shifted from a physical to a spiritual dimension. The things that you keep, which belonged to your baby twin, will be a tangible reminder of their status in your family. As we talked about in chapter one, you may have created a Memory Box for your baby twin including things like hospital cot tags, photos, foot-prints, hand-prints, locks of hair, engraved baby bracelets, teddy bears or figurines that symbolise the multiple birth status of your babies or even a set of clothes in which your babies were dressed. There are so many beautiful, tangible reminders that you can keep safely tucked away and the beauty of a Memory Box is that you can look through your baby twin's things whenever you need to.

There are two children's books which may be helpful to read to your surviving twin when they are a bit older. When they have outgrown these books, the books themselves may become another beautiful addition to your Memory Box. The books are, firstly, *Always My Twin* by Valerie Samuels. This is a beautifully written and illustrated book for young surviving twins. The second is *What is Heaven?* by Maria Shriver. For your surviving twin and other young children in your household, this book can help explain in simple terms what has happened to their sibling who has died.

Creating Something Meaningful

With time, you may find there are other things you can do to maintain your emotional bond with your baby twin. For me, these things include writing poetry and nature photography. For you, it may be composing a piece of music or writing a song, or doing something artistic like painting or making handmade jewellery or other special keepsakes. There are so many beautiful ways that you can keep the memory of your baby twin alive and remain emotionally connected to them. You just have to find whatever it is that feels right for you.

About 10 years ago my husband gave me a Canon DSLR camera and suggested I take TAFE classes to learn how to use the camera manually. This opened up a whole new world for me. I started creating a series of "roses and raindrops" images, all of which are taken in Meggie's memory. The delicate fragility and beauty of the roses reminds me of her tiny, perfectly formed body, and the raindrops are symbolic of my love and grief for her. I have a beautiful collection of roses and raindrops images and they help bring more peace into my heart.

Starting Your Own Traditions

Another way of creating meaning and finding some peace and joy to take with you through the years, is to start traditions that are unique and relevant to your household. You will find, through the years, that your baby twin will thus always have his/her special place within your family. It may seem a long way off just yet, but one day your surviving twin and his/her living siblings will be adults… and one day they will bring their partners and babies home to visit you. When this happens these traditions will be important.

What is something special you can envisage doing year-after-year together as a family? Is there a way that you can include the memory of your baby twin? It may be something as simple as wearing a piece of jewellery symbolic of your baby twin for family photos. On family-oriented days, it could be inviting everyone to bring one flower in your baby twin's memory to place in a vase and, on that day or the next, taking those flowers to the memorial gardens to lay at his/her plaque. It may be hanging a special ornament on the Christmas tree every year. The possibilities of what you could do to include your baby twin are endless – just do whatever it is that helps make you smile to know your baby twin is remembered by you and your family in a way that brings peace, not just to you, but also to your partner, your surviving twin and his/her siblings.

Creating A Legacy

Creating a legacy in your baby twin's memory is another way to keep their memory alive. It may be raising awareness of multiple birth loss, telling your story and reaching out to others. It may be finding a cause or charity that resonates with you, that you can support in your baby twin's memory. Think about how your baby twin has impacted your life and those around you. Think about what a positive difference can be made for others in a way that honours your baby twin's memory and makes your heart feel good. Think about how you might be able to influence change for the better, particularly for other grieving families in the future. Though sadly this won't change your situation, it can bring your heart joy knowing you have helped other families in a real way.

The Australian-based peer support group OzMOST has often been described by its members as Meggie's legacy to other grieving families. That wasn't so much in my thinking back in 2001 when I first established the group. At that time it was more in my thinking to make contact with other twin mums like me. As the years have gone by, though, I have often marvelled that because of Meggie, so many wonderful people have come into my life and are now life-long friends. The friendship and support we share is mutual, and OzMOST has achieved my aim of bringing people together in their shared experience of grief. That is something truly wonderful that makes my heart feel very glad.

Conclusion

From my poetry collection © 2010

*Loss teaches us so much about ourselves
and of what is really important in life.
And we discover a resilience and inner strength
we never dreamed we'd be capable of.*

I started writing this book in the week following my twins' 21st birthday. Every day of writing since that time has taken me on a journey. Some places along the way have brought with them a sense of familiarity to me that endures through the years. Other places were surprising, buried deep in my memory, resurfacing for as long as I needed to tap into them again. As well as being inspired by my own experience of twin loss, this book draws on what I now know with the benefit of hindsight and what I have learnt from observing those around me.

I'm pretty sure it hasn't escaped your attention that I have been very careful not to divulge identifying information about my surviving twin. My children are both adults now and, as such, I respect their right to privacy. To that end, I have endeavoured to keep what I have shared in this book relevant to you and where you might be in your own journey of grief and coming to understand this complicated situation of multiple birth bereavement. Whether you are a grieving parent trying to make sense of your own loss or a health care professional wanting to provide someone with guidance and reassurance, I hope this book has helped equip you with the knowledge you need for the journey ahead.

No matter where you are in your own journey of grieving and healing your broken heart from the loss of your baby twin, I hope that in some small way this book has been helpful and insightful for you. I hope it brings you comfort and reassurance to know that you are not alone in your experience. I hope it helps you draw on your own inner strength and resilience to cope day-by-day and to grieve in a way that feels natural and congruent to you. I hope it encourages you to reach out and accept the support and love that surrounds you, and to link into whatever additional support networks are available to you, wherever you are. Maybe one day you will tell me the story of your twins – I would genuinely love to hear from you.

Whilst this book has been inspired by my own personal experience of twin loss, for me it hasn't been about going back to that raw place of my own grief and sharing my story in great detail. In fact, there are so many things I have not mentioned about my own story, which is a choice I have made for many different reasons! Rather, this book is more about conveying to you, the reader, that I have been there. I want you to know that I have survived the grief and trauma of my own loss… and I want to reassure you – from one twin mum to another – that you will too.

Writing and Discussion Prompts

The following are thoughts and questions which relate to multiple birth bereavement and the nature of grief. They could be used, for example, as writing prompts for your grief journals. They could also help provide you with the opportunity for discussion around your grief with a trusted confidante, or perhaps in a peer group setting for twin loss, or even with a mental health professional. Whatever your application, I trust that they will be thought-provoking and helpful.

You and Your Grief
- What did you find helpful around the time of your twins' births?
- What was unhelpful?
- Would you do anything differently now with the benefit of hindsight?
- What would you like to say to every newly bereaved parent?
- Has the way in which you express your grief been misinterpreted by others as something else?
- What could you do for yourself that would make a difference to your healing?
- What could you do for your partner that would make a difference to their healing?
- Watching our surviving twin grow and reach milestones, we will have those "what if" moments that leave us struggling with the unanswered questions of our loss. How have you coped with those "what if" moments?

- Has a family member or friend also suffered from pregnancy loss? How did this impact on your own loss?
- Has your relationship with your family of origin changed because of your experience of loss?
- Has your loss affected your spiritual faith or beliefs? Do you question your long-held beliefs more now since your loss or has your experience of loss strengthened your faith?
- If your twins were your first pregnancy, did the thought of your surviving twin growing up as an "only child" influence your decision to try again for another baby?

Who You Are Because Of Your Grief

- Who were you before your loss? Do you miss parts of yourself pre-loss?
- What would you say to your younger self regarding your journey of grief?
- Each of us has a story to tell – what is your story?
- If you could rewrite the story of your life, would you?

Your Surviving Twin

- What are your hopes and dreams for your surviving twin?
- How can you help your surviving twin as they grow in their awareness of themselves as a "twinless twin"?
- How can you convey to your surviving twin that they are "enough" and that they won't be living in the shadow of their baby twin sibling?
- How does your relationship with your surviving twin differ to that of your other living children?

- When your surviving twin is an adult, what do you hope will be their enduring, fond memory of their own childhood?
- How do you think your surviving twin will describe their relationship with you, your partner and their other siblings (if any)?

Your Baby Twin

- If you could spend an hour with your baby twin today, what would you say to him/her?
- Have you bought or done something special in remembrance of your baby twin? It might be a piece of jewellery you wear in his/her honour, a family tradition you have started, or maybe even a tattoo.
- Is there that someone special in your life who ALWAYS remembers your baby twin and says their name to you, no matter what?

Their Special Days

- Does it make sense to you to separate the special days for honouring each of your twins?
- Often the days leading up to your twins special days are hard because of the anticipation – what can you do to make those days gentler for yourself and your household?
- What do you think will help you approach your twins' special days and other family-oriented days such as birthdays, Mothers' Day, Fathers' Day, Christmas, Easter, etc?
- If your twins were born a number of years ago, has the way you approach those special days changed through the years?

Recommended Reading

There are so many books that I have read on grief and loss over the years (too many to list below!). I have narrowed my list down to just a few that I would gladly recommend for anyone wanting to understand more about grief and healing from emotional trauma.

They are as follows:

- AZRI, Stephanie & ILSE, Sherokee. *The Prenatal Bombshell* (2015) Maryland: Rowman & Littlefield. An extremely well thought out book which guides expectant parents as they navigate their way through the devastating news of a prenatal diagnosis.
- GOLDEN, Thomas. *Swallowed By A Snake* (2nd edn, 1996) Maryland: GH Publishing LLC. Whilst written from the perspective of man-to-man, this book provides a beautiful insight for both men and women into the way in which men grieve and embark on their journey of healing.
- McKISSOCK, Mal & McKISSOCK, Dianne. *Coping With Grief* (5th edn, 2018) Sydney: HarperCollins Publishers. A very wise and thoughtful look at the nature of grief and what to expect in the early days, weeks and months following a significant loss.
- PHILLIPS, Suzanne & KANE, Dianne. *Healing Together* (2008) Oakland: New Harbinger Publications. A book to help couples come together in their grief in the

context of post-traumatic stress disorder. The authors include pregnancy loss and stillbirth in their definition of trauma. An informative, insightful and very helpful book.
- WINGARD, Barbara & LESTER, Jane. *Telling Our Stories In Ways That Make Us Stronger* (2001) Adelaide: Dulwich Centre Publications. A beautiful insight into the way in which Indigenous Australians grieve and heal from their losses.
- WORDEN, J William. *Grief Counselling and Grief Therapy* (3rd edn, 2005) Sussex: Routledge. I recommend this book especially for health/mental health professionals seeking insights into the Mediators and Tasks of Mourning, as well as disenfranchised and complicated grief.

Twin Loss Support Organisations

Australia

OzMOST – Twin Loss Support Australia
Email: OzMOST@yahoo.com
Postal: PO Box 246 Unanderra NSW 2526 Australia

New Zealand

Twin Loss NZ
Website: https://twinlossnz.wordpress.com/
Email: twinloss@xtra.co.nz

United Kingdom

Twins Trust Bereavement Support
Website: https://twinstrust.org/bereavement.html
Email: bereavementsupport@twinstrust.org

USA

CLIMB (Centre for Loss In Multiple Birth)
Website: https://www.climb-support.org/
Email: climb@climb-support.org

Part Two

For Those In a Supportive Role

From my poetry collection © 2015

We are all human.
We all love.
We will all lose something precious
to us at some point in our life.
We will all grieve.
Let's do that together.
Let's be there for each other.

In my introduction, I mentioned that this book has been written not just for grieving parents but also as a guide to help their social and professional supports in understanding the complicated nature of multiple birth bereavement. You may be the parent, grandparent, brother, sister, aunt, uncle, niece, nephew, cousin, close friend or work colleague of the bereaved parents. I have written this chapter for you.

Whatever your relationship to the grieving parents, they are important to you and the death of their baby twin is also an important loss for you to grieve. You will be aware that your relationship with the baby twin who has died differs to that of the grieving parents and their other children, because of the strong emotional bond they have already established with both of their babies. You dearly want to reach out and support them, but you're not sure how to do that or of even what they need. So let's take a look at the role which others can play in offering their support to grieving parents.

Close Social Supports

The death of a loved one has a way of bringing people together even when their paths may not necessarily otherwise have crossed. How many times have you attended a funeral and heard someone say, "I wish we were meeting again under happier circumstances"? At such times of sadness, we are united in our loss and grief, and that's exactly what we need.

There seems to be an unspoken rule, that once a funeral is over the public grieving ends. However, if you have ever experienced the death of someone you loved dearly, you will know that your grief lasted long after the funeral ended. In fact, in many circumstances of loss, at the time of the funeral the real grieving hadn't yet even begun.

In twin pregnancies like mine, where an unborn twin dies, the shock of the loss and the grieving begins before the birth. This can leave twin parents feeling quite vulnerable and helpless. Thankfully, this is also a time when many people will gather around them and offer their condolences and best wishes for the remainder of the pregnancy. There may also be offers of practical help around the house and with their other children.

I want to acknowledge that being there and offering to help is not easy to do when you, like your grieving loved ones, also feel quite helpless and are in shock over the death of their baby twin. You may also be needing to have some time and space to adjust to this sad family news. You may worry, as you do this, that you seem distant or even uncaring. Let me assure you that if you have a good, solid relationship with the grieving parents, then they will likely understand you are also coming to terms with their loss and struggling to know how to help.

The challenge for anyone in a close, supportive role to grieving parents is in helping to empower them to make their own decisions. As we saw in chapter one, grieving parents will face many decisions around the impending live birth and stillbirth of their twins – things that they have to consider which, days or weeks earlier, were not even on their radar. Decisions will need to be made around the birth of both babies and also with regard to memory making. Parents may have to make heart-breaking decisions around whether or not to proceed with an autopsy, making arrangements for the funeral, and even choosing an outfit for their baby twin to wear in his/her coffin. These decisions may seem too hard or overwhelming and grieving parents may struggle with wondering if they are doing the right thing. Any decision that they have to make will be based on the information that has been made available to them at that time. Having a good network of support around them will thus be very reassuring.

This is not a situation where someone else can intervene and make these decisions on the parents' behalf. Doing this would only make them feel even more vulnerable – remember, their baby twin's death occurred in a situation over which they had little or no control. The decisions they are faced with are something that no expectant parent should have to contend with and yet, ultimately, only they can make them.

Attending Appointments

As an expectant twin mum, your loved one will likely have weekly appointments now to monitor both her health and the surviving twin's well-being as the pregnancy progresses. One very practical way in which you can be supportive is by offering to attend those appointments with her, if her partner is not able to do so. This can be helpful for many different reasons. On the way to/from the appointments, there is the opportunity to talk things over. The parents may have questions they need to ask and it might be helpful to have those questions written down so they don't have to worry about forgetting to mention important things. You can be helpful in remembering things too. Most importantly, your presence and support may be very comforting and reassuring for her.

As I look back to my own twin pregnancy, I think the hardest thing by far was dealing with the unknowns. Always in my thinking was the obstetrician's advice on that dark day of my mid-pregnancy sonogram, for me to go home and prepare myself mentally for the premature stillbirth of both my twins. It was always a huge relief just to make it to my next weekly appointment at the hospital prenatal clinic. I was literally living from one week to the next and it became my goal simply to make it to the next weekly appointment. I was thankful for each day my unborn surviving twin continued to grow and remain healthy. As the pregnancy neared term he was an active little thing and to feel him kicking and moving was so very reassuring to me that we just might make it to full-term after all.

With each weekly appointment I often had questions to ask the Registrar, who I found to be very approachable and kind. At that time, my husband was working 12-hour shifts and with a 3-hour daily commute, he wasn't available to attend those appointments with me. Most times I would write my questions down so that I wouldn't forget to ask about the things that were making me anxious. My BP reading was typically quite high and there was almost always the discussion of admitting me for complete bed-rest. On one particular occasion, just a few weeks off my twins being born, I was so anxious that I could barely speak. I had my questions written down, but I couldn't bring myself to ask them. To have my husband with me on that particular day would have made a huge difference to my anxiety levels – thankfully, my mother was able to step into the role as my support person for my final hospital prenatal check-up appointment.

The Need To Talk

It may take a few years following their loss for your loved ones to work through the depth of their grief, as they seek to make sense of it all. As an ongoing part of this process, they may need to talk about their experience several times over and it requires time and care to support the grieving parents through this. Have you ever said something out loud and realised, as you hear yourself speak, that your thoughts suddenly came into sharp focus? There is power in the spoken word.

Sometimes hearing ourselves say something out loud can bring with it clarity, a new understanding, a realisation, an epiphany. In acute grief, there are many such moments that arise from a deep and ongoing need to talk about the loss over and over again.

When a grieving person does this, the telling their story of loss several times over helps them to understand it more and it also helps to decrease the intensity of their feelings over time. This is a slow process. It really does take a long time; however, it is also a necessary process that helps grieving parents make sense of it all. In order to do that, they need a strong network of support around them.

Support happens when we give of ourselves and our time. The most powerful gift you can give to your grieving loved one is yourself. You don't have to jump in and fill the silences with your words. You don't have to have all of the answers. You don't have to have a degree in psychology to know what to say. Just follow their lead. Try to imagine what it would be like if the roles were reversed and you were in their situation. There may be times when there are no words and that's okay. You just have to be there.

The Need To Cry

The nature of grief is such that when we are sad, we cry. Grief can make you feel almost child-like again and in that way, it can be emotionally very regressive. I have thought about this a lot through the years and my one enduring thought about why we feel this way is that grief puts us in a position of needing to be looked after. We need to be comforted. We need to be heard. We need to be reassured.

I also want to acknowledge that there's a real sense of helplessness in watching someone you love go through a trauma and sitting with them, allowing them to be in their grief. Watching them cry can make you feel very emotional too. Those tears can come from a place of empathy because in that moment you may have a sense of what it is like to be in their situation, living with their experience of trauma and grief hour-by-hour and day-by-day. When a situation is so far outside of your frame of reference, it can be hard to know how to react and how to help. You may struggle with knowing what to say that will be of help. Just remember that there are three very important words that can make a world of difference: "Help me understand…"

When we are comforting someone, we have to resist the urge to stop them from crying, because in doing so we stop them from expressing their emotional pain. Without even realising it, we may interrupt their crying by touching their arm or saying something. We may be tempted to do this to ease our discomfort in being around them while they are in such a state of distress. However, stopping a grieving person from crying can leave them feeling misunderstood and subsequently also frustrated – and there no comfort in that. There are another three words that can go a long way towards helping a grieving person to express themselves: "Take your time…" These three words are a good reminder to just sit with them in their pain and not try to "fix" anything for them. Sometimes sitting quietly with them is all we need to do.

A Loss Is A Loss Is A Loss

Words are powerful and we can use them to build a person up or to tear a person down. When it comes to our long held beliefs about pregnancy loss and stillbirth, we need to think very carefully about the words we use when speaking about the baby who has died, as well as when we are talking to grieving parents. When people first hear about a tragic event such as the death of an unborn child, they may be tempted to compare the parents' loss with other people's losses or perhaps even their own past experiences. Yet, when a grieving parents' loss is compared to that of another person's experience, it begs the question: Is the intention to make them feel bad for grieving because the other person's loss is somehow perceived as "bigger" than theirs? As I write this, I would hope that's not the intention, however, this is how it may be interpreted.

Remember that the parents had already started to develop a deep emotional bond with their unborn babies and, in their thinking, both twins were already an important part of their anticipated future. Their grief is both the sadness and love they experience at a significant loss. Their baby twin who has died was important to them. He/she meant the world to them. As tragic as those other losses may be, the loss grieving parents' feel cannot be compared with another person's experience. A loss is a loss is a loss. And for the parents, that loss is profound.

As a mum who carried her baby twin dead for the second half of the pregnancy, I had people belittle my loss. Some people even tried to convince me I was no longer pregnant with twins (I learnt the hard way not to throw my pearls to the swine!).

Having also experienced miscarriage and the loss of several other babies through the IVF process leading up to my twin pregnancy, I do have to say that the gestational age of a baby at death is not relevant to grieving parents.

The death of an unborn baby is no less of a loss than a full-term stillbirth or if a child dies in infancy or early childhood. Each person's experience is unique to them. Each and every loss is profound in the individual parents' eyes and each one is a loss that needs to be both acknowledged and grieved.

Extended Social Circles

Within your own social circles, take extra care when talking to other people about the grieving parents' circumstance of loss. Be mindful of how vulnerable they are at this time. It is not always appropriate to talk to other people about the details of someone else's loss and grief – grieving parents need to know that they can trust you to keep the confidentiality between you and them. It is their prerogative to decide who they want to confide in about the more private aspects of their grief.

Instead, when other friends and family members ask after them encourage these people to make contact with the grieving parents personally. If you get caught in the middle, relaying information back and forth to others, you run the risk of the intended support of others being inadvertently misdirected away from the grieving parents.

People generally ask questions because they care, but just be mindful that it is the grieving parents who need to hear those words of care and concern directly. It often means the world to grieving parents to receive a text message, an email, a note in the letterbox or a phone call offering support. Rather than being told that others are being supportive, they need to feel and experience that support for themselves and when that happens, they will subsequently have a greater sense of the wealth of support from those who have gathered around them.

Making contact doesn't have to require a lot of effort and these small gestures of kindness in reaching out will go a long way towards lessening any feelings of being disconnected. If ever grieving parents need to have a strong sense of the support from everyone around them, it will be now. They need your words of comfort and reassurance. Let them hear them.

When The Supporter Needs Support

It is not easy being in a supportive role, watching someone you love dearly go through such a deeply traumatising experience. Please know that the National Helplines (as mentioned in chapter three) are also there for you, if you think it might be helpful to elicit some extra support for yourself.

Additionally, you could also talk to your GP with a view to talking to a grief counsellor as well. You may find it helps a lot to talk to someone who has a specialised knowledge of grief and of child loss.

Misinterpreting Grief

Sometimes grief can be misinterpreted as something that it isn't and I think that is because, in the very specific situation of twin loss, there is a newborn baby thrown into the mix. In my introduction, I made the comment that the sight of a mother holding a newborn baby isn't normally the image we have of grief. In every other context, this image is one of joy and hope and celebration – and it still is that for the surviving twin. However, there is an added layer of grief which can be so easily misunderstood.

Anyone in a supportive role should encourage grieving parents to express their emotions in a safe and healthy way. Care also needs to be taken when considering their mental well-being – it is not yours to question their mental health. Remember, you are there in a supportive role only.

However, if you have any concerns, think of kind and gentle ways to encourage them to link into professional supports such as a grief counsellor or psychologist to elicit any extra support they need and deserve.

When grieving parents feel misunderstood and judged by others, it can add a burden of unnecessary grief for them and leave them feeling frustrated and angry. It takes the focus away from their grief and it can be damaging for their interpersonal relationships. It also takes away the emotional safety that grieving parents need to have around them. Keep it in your thinking that their emotional expression of grief isn't always going to be as intense as it is in the first few years of their loss. For now, while their grief is this intense and raw, they just need you to love them through it. And while you do, they are coping the only way they know how.

Let's have a look at the ways in which grief may not be recognised as such, so that we can have a better understanding of what the parents' grief is and what they might need from you.

Grief Misconstrued As Not Coping

"How would you have coped with two babies?" These are the words that every grieving multiple birth parent dreads hearing. The harsh truth is, they never got to know how they would have coped with two babies. Instead, their reality is dealing with the round-the-clock demands of a newborn baby, and occurring parallel to that is their experience of profound grief and loss.

When you notice that the grieving parents seem sad and overly tired, remember that they are dealing with both of these realities simultaneously. In your eyes, they may not seem to be coping. In their eyes, they are doing the best they can to get through from one day to the next.

It may be that their surviving twin is unsettled through the night and they are trying to cope with broken sleep and establishing a good day/night routine with him/her. If they have other children, those children will also be grieving the loss of their baby brother/sister and their parents are supporting them through this.

As a couple and as a family, they are all grieving both individually and together as their entire household adjusts to their "new normal" on a day-to-day basis. It may be that as time goes on and they process their loss more, that they experience the pain of their grief even more intensely.

I daresay you can confidently claim you don't know of anyone else in your circles of family and friends who have gone through what the grieving parents are living and experiencing with their twin loss. Learn to recognise their grief for what it is and see this perhaps as an opportunity to ask what they might need in terms of practical help.

Grief Misconstrued As Being Negative

Feeling sad should not be confused with being negative, so imploring grieving parents to think positively sends the message that they're not "allowed" to be sad about their baby twin when in the company of certain people.

Feeling misinterpreted and misunderstood in such a way creates a risk that the grieving parents might build a wall of self-preservation around themselves. They might seek to establish a safe distance between themselves and the words and opinions of others. You can't ever really know what they are thinking and feeling. Keeping an open mind will help build a more meaningful understanding between you and them.

Looking through the eyes of grieving parents, what could possibly be a positive about their baby twin dying? I can't think of anything. Can you? A person with a negative outlook on life will consistently notice and focus on the bad things about mostly everything and, I am guessing, that this mindset may be longstanding. The sad feelings resulting from such a profound loss is very different to a mindset of negativity. Remember, sadness is an integral part of expressing grief.

Grief Misconstrued As Jealousy

One thing that grieving parents will likely also encounter following their loss are the pregnancies with happy outcomes of family and friends in their extended circles. I've heard it said many times through the years, "One of my greatest fears is someone I know falling pregnant with twins".

It's not outside the realms of possibility for this to happen and it is a situation where grieving parents will need additional support and lots of understanding and care. Their fear is twofold:

on the one hand, of something going wrong with this new twin pregnancy (that is, after all, their personal experience) and on the other hand, of having to watch someone in their extended circles raise an intact set of twins (their shattered dream).

At such times the grieving parents will be reminded of their twin pregnancy pre-loss and the excitement and joy that surrounded them at that time – and, at the same time, they will also be reminded of the subsequent sadness following their loss.

Although they still define themselves as the parents of twins, this is a time where they will feel quite keenly their "social" loss of status as the parents of twins. They will likely struggle with these conflicting memories and will need to invest a lot of emotional energy into being happy for their loved ones, despite their own personal sadness and deep sense of yearning and longing. Sometimes, however, that sadness will be the one emotion they can't help but express.

Rather than misinterpreting their sadness as jealousy, understand that at times like this they will be missing their baby twin just that little bit more – their hearts will be aching just that little bit more.

Acknowledge that this is a real struggle for them. Try to imagine what it would be like to be in their shoes. Be mindful that they will always feel sad about their baby twin who has died and that this happy time for others – where everyone around them is celebrating – is a reminder that they will always grieve for what will never be for their twins.

Minimising Grief

We also need to be aware of the ways in which the parents' grief may be minimised or underestimated. As time progresses, they will have their good days and their bad days. When we talk to them about their grief and loss we need to be very careful with the words we choose because, once they are spoken, there is no taking them back.

Grief, I have found, has a very long memory. Just as we remember all of the beautiful, kind words spoken to us that brought comfort and soothed our soul, we also remember with clarity the words and moments that cut like a knife, breaking our hearts and leaving us feeling wounded, violated and vulnerable all over again.

You're Just Upset

In the context of being upset, I mean being agitated, frustrated, even angry. There is always a reason why we feel and respond to situations in the way we do. Our feelings may stem from the frustration of being misunderstood. It may be that we don't feel validated in our loss or well supported. When people say that the grieving parents were "just upset", they need to be careful not to minimise their grief. Unless you have also gone through an experience of twin loss, you can't possibly understand the depth of grief and the struggle it is some days just to get through. Remember, our grief is there because of our love and, with the loss of a baby (even an unborn baby), that love is deep. As we saw in chapter two, grief expresses itself in a range of difficult emotions and your grieving loved ones may experience all of these as they work through the maze of their own feelings and adjust to their loss in their own way and time. These are not easy feelings to experience and work through, but they are a necessary part of grief.

You're Feeling Sorry For Yourself

The grieving parents may be described as being self-indulgent, as wallowing in self-pity, as feeling sorry for themselves. It might help to understand this instead as the all-consuming aspect of their grief. If you have ever experienced a significant loss you will remember that, for a time, your loss and grief were in the forefront of your thinking. When you woke in the morning, that second you became aware, your grief was there… and it would be the last thing you thought of as you went to sleep at night. Your grief would be there with every waking thought in between. You couldn't help it; it was just that important to you. In a similar way, that's what the grieving parents are going through. Just consider how profound their loss is and the hard work emotionally they have to do to be at peace with it. And remember, in those first few years they have a huge need to talk about their loss and express their sadness.

You're Just Being Selfish:

For the first few years, during acute grief, the grieving parents likely will be focused almost exclusively on themselves and their household. Understandably, their focus will be on their surviving twin and other living children. Their focus will also be on their baby twin who has died… and their own grieving process, of trying to find a way to heal both individually and together. Much of their grieving will be done in private. Grief cannot be rushed or pushed to the side. It cannot be suppressed and you cannot just "get over it" in the space of a few weeks or months (the truth is, the grieving parents won't ever "get over it").

It needs to be understood that for a while, they will have little energy or time for the more peripheral aspects of their lives. They are not being selfish – this is all a part of their survival. While they are surviving the waves of their grief, you can support them through your patience and understanding.

Other Things to Be Aware Of

Defaulting To Clichés

I have often wondered why people default to clichés such as "your baby is in a better place now". I think it stems from people not knowing what else to say and perhaps wanting to move the conversation on to something they feel more comfortable talking about.

They may also not have any self-awareness about the impact of their words. No matter what your or their beliefs about life, death and religion are – what could possibly be a better place for a baby than in his/her parents' arms? Surely not their ashes in an urn.

Saying their baby is in a "better" place conveys the message to the parents that, even though their baby twin has died, you're okay with that. Other clichés include: "It was for the best", "It wasn't meant to be" and even "Be grateful for what you have". Clichés like these will come across as cruel and callous to grieving parents.

Rather than defaulting to these and other clichés, perhaps consider that the words, "I'm sorry, I just don't know what to say" is all you need to say.

Pregnancies Don't Come With Guarantees

While the grieving parents are awaiting the birth of their twins, it can be tempting to give them false hope. You may believe with all your heart that the surviving twin will make it to term and be born alive and healthy. Of course, that is the outcome everyone hopes for.

However, as much as you want this to be the reality – and to encourage the parents to believe that too – there are no guarantees. Being healthy is no guarantee. Having a strong faith is no guarantee.

Having the best care in the country is no guarantee. The grieving parents have already experienced the fragility of life and death and how everything can change in an instant. One of their unborn twins has already died. As much as you want to, you can't guarantee that their other twin will survive.

In a similar way, you also cannot guarantee that they will fall pregnant again in the future and have a better outcome "next time". Because of my primary infertility, it took several years for us to conceive our babies. Other couples may experience secondary infertility following their first pregnancy. For them, there may not be a "next time".

The most powerful thing you can do is hold the hand of the grieving parents and hope alongside them. Share their sadness. Validate their loss. Listen to their fears. Acknowledge that nobody will have all of the answers.

Encourage them to focus on grieving and grieving well. Commit to supporting them emotionally for as long as they need your support. And remind them that there is still hope and to hold onto that… together.

Traditions In The Extended Family Circles

It is important to be aware of not placing unrealistic expectations onto grieving parents, especially around the significant dates of their twins (for example, their twins' birthday and the anniversary of their baby twin's death).

Remember that they have an emotional bond with their baby twin that is unique to them and, as a family unit, they may be starting their own traditions for memorialising. This emotional bond will endure through the years.

Regardless of what other family-oriented events may also occur around the same time as their twins' special dates, be mindful that grieving parents need to honour each of their twins in their own way and time, and that this is an important part of their grieving process. Whether they choose to involve others or prefer to do things privately is entirely up to them.

Grieving parents may feel guilty if undue pressure is placed on them to participate in other extended family-oriented occasions before they are ready, as they always had prior to their loss, although this isn't your intention. Their focus shouldn't be on trying to keep everyone around them happy and the more an issue is made of something, the more of an issue it is likely to become.

Be mindful that their whole world has changed now and something tragic has occurred that they hadn't, in a million years, anticipated would happen to them. Nobody did. Be patient with them – realistically it could take a few years for them to adjust and re-enter their wider social circles again. Grief doesn't exist within the confines of time.

Let it be on the grieving parents' terms to decide when they feel emotionally ready to be involved again. Let it be on their terms how they negotiate their ongoing involvement with their extended circles in future years. They will appreciate you giving them the time and space they need to adjust to their loss, and to rejoin the wider family and social circles when they feel they are ready.

Keep Your Focus On The Relationships

As I have been considering the various points in this chapter, my prevailing thought is of the importance of maintaining healthy relationships. As families grow and evolve, so too do the ways they express their interpersonal relationships with one another. Children grow up and leave their family of origin, making a life for themselves and living with their own sense of autonomy and purpose in life. We raise our children to be adults, after all. In this same way, the grieving parents may have forged their own independence from you and merged their lives together to create their own family unit. Through the years, that cycle of growing and evolving will continue through their children… and their children's children.

There will always be changes that we have to adjust to during our lives. That's life. At some point or other, we start to realise what is really important to us. As a consequence of that, some of the more peripheral aspects of our lives will "give".

When we go through a traumatic experience, as we process and understand it more, what is (and isn't) important to us comes into sharp focus. This is a good reminder to keep your relationship with them as a priority. Yes, some things will change for them. Some things will change for you. Some of those changes may be temporary.

Others may be more long-term. We each have to commit to taking our life in the direction that is right for us and taking steps towards our own equilibrium in the long-term. If the foundation of your relationship with them is a strong one, then it will withstand those changes and it will grow stronger because of those changes. That's the one thing you don't want to change – the strength of your relationship with them.

Be the One Who Remembers

If there is anything that is music to a grieving parent's ears then it is hearing their baby twin's name spoken out loud. As time goes by, especially with the passage of many years, the large majority of people in their extended circles will (sadly) remain silent about the baby twin who has died.

It's not that they have forgotten, but just that they may not realise just how much it means to grieving parents to have those ongoing acknowledgements – especially on occasions such as the twins' birthday and the anniversary of the baby twin's death.

Some people will worry that mentioning the name of the baby twin will upset the parents. Let me assure you that it won't. Yes, the parents may become emotional, however, they are not upset. They are, quite simply, touched that you have shown them you remember too.

I hope that every grieving parent will be able to say they have one person, just one person, in their lives who will always remember to say their baby twin's name out loud. I have had one special person in my life like that. I want to encourage you to be that person for your loved ones.

Acknowledgements

My sincere thanks goes to John, who has always supported me with unwavering love, and to Tom and Ellis, who have grown into amazing men and of whom we love dearly and are so very proud.

In addition, I am ever so grateful to the following people:

My dear friend Jon, who sowed the seed of a thought that I may, one day, write a book.

My life-long friend David, who challenged me with the words, "When you set your heart on something, you get it done". You have always believed in me and I thank you for cheering me on from the sidelines through every week of writing.

Julie-Anne Geddes for her ongoing support, for her wise and thoughtful feedback and for the care put into writing the Foreword to this book.

Philippa Findlay and Sarah Plant of Puddingburn Publishing Services NSW for their excellence in proofing the manuscript and for their kind, encouraging words.

Kev Howlett and Les Zigomanis of Busybird Publishing VIC for their expertise in taking my manuscript and transforming it into a book I can be very proud of. From day one I knew it was in good hands with you.

Lastly, but certainly not least, to my OzMOST friends – too many to name individually, but you know who you are. The experiences we have shared takes our understanding of twin loss way beyond empathy. We have travelled many a mile together through the years and I love you like family.

About the Author

Julie Ann, together with her husband and their two adult children, lives in the Illawarra NSW Australia – a region traditionally known as Dharawal Country, the land of the Wodi Wodi people. She works from home as a medical transcriptionist in radiology.

When her children were young, Julie Ann completed the Advanced Diploma of Applied Social Science. Her studies focused on grief and loss, and she has a specific interest in disenfranchised grief, especially as it relates to multiple birth bereavement.

Julie Ann's other interests include listening to music, writing poetry – a few of her poems are shared in this book – and nature photography.

To subscribe to Julie Ann's regular blogs on multiple birth bereavement, visit her website:

https://fromonetwinmumtoanother.com/

www.ingramcontent.com/pod-product-compliance
Lightning Source LLC
Chambersburg PA
CBHW030302100526
44590CB00012B/487